GRADUATE RESEARCH

A Guide
for Students
in the
Sciences

Third Edition

Robert V. Smith

University of Washington Press • Seattle and London

Copyright © 1998 by the University of Washington Press
First edition, 1984; second edition, 1990; third edition, revised and expanded,
published by the University of Washington Press in 1998.

13 12 11 10 09 08 07 06   8 7 6 5 4 3

University of Washington Press
PO Box 50096
Seattle, WA 98145-5096
www.washington.edu/uwpress

Designed and produced by Laing Communications Inc., Redmond, Washington
Printed in the United States of America

Library of Congress Cataloging-in-Publication Data
Smith, Robert V. 1942–
Graduate Research: a guide for students in the sciences / Robert V. Smith—
3rd ed., rev. and expanded.
    Bibliography: p.   cm.
    Includes index.
    ISBN 0-295-97705-1
1. Research—Methodology.   I. Title.
Q180.55.M4S58   1998   001.4'2—dc21   98-4845

The paper used in this publication meets the minimum requirements of American
National Standard for Information Sciences—Permanence of Paper for Printed
Library Materials, ANSI Z39.48-1984. ∞

GRADUATE RESEARCH

A Guide
for Students
in the
Sciences

Third Edition

To the Daughter of Mars

CONTENTS

PREFACE

. . . in a scientific laboratory, nothing startling which calls for an obvious response occurs on its own. Nature is passive and silent. Scientists have to start things up for themselves.

—June Goodfield

Research and scholarship are the lifeblood of society. Professionals in many different fields at one time or another will have to conduct research, but it is crucial for graduate students in the sciences to master this skill. Their careers depend on it.

A worrisome paradox lurks in graduate education. At this level, more than any other, the student must develop independence and creativity. Consequently, advisors are likely to adopt a laissez-faire attitude toward the student's work. This may cause the student to struggle unnecessarily. Guidance is needed to excel in research.

The problems of developing and improving research skills and preparing for professional careers are addressed in this book. It is a step-by-step guide for students in the life, natural, physical, and social-behavioral sciences. It can also benefit faculty or administrators who wish to organize their thinking on graduate education. The book is designed for self-instruction. It could serve as a reference for an introductory research methods course or departmental seminar. The book was also conceived as a work that might be offered by an advisor to a beginning graduate student as an "introductory reading," accompanied by the suggestion, "After you have read this book, we should discuss how its guidelines may help you progress in our program."

The book is succinct and can be read quickly, but hints are offered that can be helpful for years. The tips given have been refined through the experiences of noted scientists and educators. The ideas will work if given a try.

I have advised graduate students as professor, director of an interdisciplinary research institute, academic dean, and graduate school dean at two research universities. Before entering administration, I directed research and published papers in various disciplines including chemistry, microbiology, and pharmacological sciences. I understand the difficulties graduate students experience in research and graduate education. Problems that stem from a lack of knowledge in course work and in specific research methods, as in statistics or computer sciences, are beyond the scope of this book. Rather, impediments involving approaches, perceptions, and self-initiating efforts are its concerns.

The book is developed in chronological fashion for the beginning graduate student. The first chapter contains an orientation to graduate research departments. It is followed by chapters on commitments and creativity, making choices (e.g., research problems and an advisor), and managing time. These are followed by chapters on the principles of scientific research and ethics in science. Subsequent chapters are devoted to library research, writing skills, preparing theses and dissertations, and presenting and publishing papers. The book continues with chapters on research with human subjects, animals, and biohazards, and on writing and applying for grants. A concluding chapter provides insights on getting a job in higher education, government, or industry.

Beginning graduate students can use this book throughout their academic careers. More advanced students may refine their skills through its use. In short, this guide should make research a more rewarding and interesting experience.

Many people helped make this book possible. Some people stimulated ideas. Others helped in the refinement of ideas and concepts. Still others were sources of encouragement. Most have been colleagues or students at the University of Michigan, the University of Iowa, the University of Texas at Austin, Washington State University, and the University of Washington. I am grateful to many individuals for their wisdom and kindness, especially to Faye Dong and her graduate students, and colleagues at the University of Washington and University of Tennessee, who encouraged the development of this edition of Graduate Research. Also, I am grateful to Vickie Croft (Washington State University), who provided essential counsel on the development of Chapter 7 on Library and Literature Work.

Finally, I wish to acknowledge my wife, Marsha June Day, who continually inspires me to look at reality in new ways.

January 1998

INTRODUCTION

What research universities value most [is] the active engagement between graduate faculty members and graduate students at the frontiers of traditional fields, where new discoveries, new perspectives, new syntheses fundamentally reorder the state of knowledge.

—John D'Arms

Research and graduate education are linked inextricably. Thus, it is not surprising that the nation's great graduate schools are located at research universities where exceptional faculty and graduate students discover and develop new knowledge.

The recruitment of outstanding graduate students is the goal of all research universities. In reciprocal fashion, prospective graduate students should seek programs that will help them become competitive in their chosen fields. The prospective student can do much to ensure a suitable match. The basis for the match should include personal interests, the quality of faculty advisors and programs, the levels of financial support, and quality of life in and around institutions.

Personal interests will influence the choice of a field of study; however, prospective graduate students should realize that graduate research and scholarship are not always represented in undergraduate courses or programs. For example, one rarely sees undergraduate courses in chemical physics or pharmacology, which are recognized doctoral areas of study.

Undergraduate advisors, faculty, and staff at a graduate school of one's alma mater are good sources for information on graduate programs. Additionally, guides are available that provide general information on graduate programs in the United States.[1-3] Once a field of study is chosen, faculty, department chairpersons, and deans at a home institution can be contacted for opinions and evaluations. For doctoral study, it is also useful to consult the latest review (conducted every 10 years) of programs evaluated through the National Research Council.[4-5] Faculty, chairpersons, and deans may also know alumni who reside in your area.

Following local inquiries, contacts should be made with potentially desirable programs. For prospective graduate students who are currently undergraduates, the following timetable may be useful in planning the inquiry, application, and evaluation steps.

Junior Year

- Determine programs and universities of interest
- Register for Graduate Record Exam (GRE; quantitative, verbal, and analytical exams; in some instances, subject tests)
- Investigate national scholarships/fellowships (see Chapter 12)

Summer between Junior and Senior Years

- Take GRE exam(s)
- Write for admission materials
- Visit institutions
- Write application essay, including motivation and commitments, expectations, experience, background, goals, reasons for pursuing graduate education, and personal uniqueness; obtain critiques of essay
- Check application deadlines and register for national application or data assembly service

Senior Year

- Obtain letters of recommendation
- Take GRE if necessary
- Send in applications (preferably 10 to 12 months in advance of starting graduate work, or as required)
- Continue visits to institutions
- Evaluate offers of admission and assistantship or fellowship support (see Chapter 3)

Admission criteria vary, but graduate schools and graduate programs generally look for a minimum B average in upper division work (typically the last 60 semester hours or 90 quarter hours), acceptable performance on the GRE (e.g., often a score of more than 500 or high national percentile ranking on the quantitative, verbal, and analytical portions of the standard exams), favorable letters of recommendation, and evidence of motivation and commitment to graduate study in a chosen area. These factors may be evaluated, in part, through interview trips sponsored by graduate programs that provide travel support as part of their recruitment efforts. The opportunity to interview is valuable, especially if it includes interviews with prospective advisors and students currently in a program.

Acceptance of admission into a graduate program should offer exciting challenges and opportunities to pursue research at the forefront of knowledge. The challenges and opportunities will require a good start, which is considered in the chapter that follows.

References

[1] *The Official* GRE/CGS *Directory of Graduate Programs*, 14th ed., Vol. A, *Natural Sciences*; Vol. B, *Engineering and Business*; Vol. C, *Social Sciences and Education* (Princeton, NJ: Educational Testing Service, 1993).

[2] ASEE's *1994–95 Directory of Engineering Graduate Studies and Research* (Washington, DC: American Society for Engineering Education, 1994).

[3] *Peterson's Graduate and Professional Programs—An Overview*, 1997, 31st ed. (Princeton, NJ: Peterson's Guides, 1997).

[4] The National Research Council represents, collectively, the National Academy of Sciences, the National Academy of Engineering, and the Institute of Medicine.

[5] M. L. Goldberger, B. A. Maher, and P. E. Flattau, eds., *Research-Doctorate Programs in the United States—Continuity and Change* (Washington, D.C.: National Academy Press, 1995). See also: http://www.nap.edu/readingroom/books/researchdoc/

GRADUATE RESEARCH

A Guide
for Students
in the
Sciences

Third Edition

1 | GETTING STARTED

Exultation is the going
Of an inland soul to sea,—
Past the houses, past the headlands,
Into deep eternity!

Bred as we, among the mountains.
Can the sailor understand
The divine intoxication
Of the first league out from land?

—Emily Dickinson

Entering graduate school marks a turning point in many lives. Graduate education is designed for individual development and growth. With commitment, hard work, and some guidance, students become independent scholars and researchers. Beginning a graduate career, however, requires knowing who's who and what's what in a graduate research unit and university.

University Organization

Universities are divided into schools and colleges. Thus, a university like Washington State University has Colleges of Agriculture and Home Economics, Business and Economics, Education, Engineering and Architecture, Liberal Arts, Nursing, Pharmacy, Sciences, and Veterinary Medicine. Additionally, there are schools of Architecture, Communication, Mechanical and Materials Engineering, and Music and Theater Arts, along with the Graduate School. Colleges and schools are headed by deans, or sometimes, in the case of the latter, directors, who most often administer a series of departments, which in turn are administered by department chairpersons. Certain smaller colleges or schools (i.e., 50 faculty members or less) may function dually as a collegiate unit and department. This means that the dean of the smaller college or school also serves as department chairperson. In addition to colleges (schools) and departments, interdisciplinary gradu-

3

ate programs and units (e.g., institutes, centers, and laboratories) may be organized through faculty from different academic areas.

Noteworthy graduate programs require outstanding faculty—faculty who have national or international reputations in research and scholarship. "Critical masses" of faculty are also necessary for excellence in graduate education. For example, chemistry departments in doctoral-granting institutions need faculty in subdisciplines such as analytical, biological, inorganic, organic, and physical chemistry. Accordingly, first-class doctoral-granting chemistry departments commonly have 30 to 50 full-time faculty representing subspecialties such as the ones noted.

As large as such a departmental faculty may seem, alone it is inadequate to ensure high quality because the best graduate (especially doctoral) programs include course requirements in other areas. Continuing with the example of chemistry, doctoral students in this discipline commonly take advanced work in fields such as biology, computer science, mathematics, and physics. The latter courses, in addition to the core work in chemistry, form foundations of excellent chemistry programs, and these in turn serve as foundations for the work and further development of graduates over many years of professional life. Analogous cross-disciplinary offerings are important in many doctoral programs from biology to horticulture to materials engineering. Additionally, future graduate professionals will increasingly require research skills in more than one discipline.

Cross-disciplinary and interdisciplinary programs offer unusual opportunities for graduate students. Indeed, the student graduating with a combined major may have a competitive career edge over one who is grounded in a single field. One can imagine, for example, unique career opportunities for mechanical-civil engineering, biochemistry-pharmacology, and computer science–psychology majors. These kinds of options may be possible through formally organized cross-disciplinary programs (possibly involving a formal minor) or through individual interdisciplinary programs available through the graduate school. If such options seem attractive, they should be explored early in one's graduate career.

Graduate schools and colleges are uniquely organized. These units have a dean and perhaps associate and assistant deans, but they have no departments. Rather, the graduate school provides an umbrella organization for all graduate programs on campus.

The graduate school serves a number of quality assurance functions for graduate programs. Through faculty committees and councils, graduate programs are initially reviewed and recommended for approval by the board of governors or regents of the university. Faculty panels and the graduate school dean are also responsible for the approval of courses, periodic review of programs, and the appointment of graduate faculty. Appointment criteria typically include an appropriate terminal degree, research productivity, and graduate-level experience in teaching, dissertation or thesis direction, or dissertation or thesis committee membership. The graduate faculty, in turn, are responsible for the day-to-day supervision of graduate students. Department chairpersons or specially designated graduate advisors are representatives of the graduate dean in departments, and these representatives are responsible for administering graduate school policies and standards. Oversight of standards, policies, and procedures is accomplished through the graduate deans and their staff, who should be available to students who have concerns about department or program advisors or programs.

The primary mission of graduate research departments is to help develop outstanding scholars and researchers. High-quality departments promote individual freedom, the vigorous pursuit of knowledge, and passion for research. First-rate departments ring with intellectual excitement—their faculties are anxious to help students execute individual plans of study which include research and scholarship at the forefront of knowledge as well as the development of professional skills. The individualized attention and approach set graduate study apart from baccalaureate and professional programs.

While students are expected to work with advisors in designing customized programs, departmental or interdisciplinary program requirements for core courses, foreign language skills, and candidacy have to be met according to program guidelines. Learn these guidelines as soon as possible. If available, obtain the department's or program's guidebook for graduate students. Also, obtain copies of the graduate school catalog and the policies and procedures manual. Make sure that descriptions in both documents can be reconciled. Direct questions to a graduate advisor or faculty member who may be assigned as a temporary advisor. Try to establish quickly how much input students have at each step of their degree programs.

The Players

Various faculty and staff are encountered during the first few weeks in a graduate research department or program. The faculty typically consists of professors (also referred to as full professors), associate professors, assistant professors, instructors, and teaching assistants. Professors generally have the greatest seniority and may hold an endowed professorship or chair, which is acknowledged by a named title. For example, the late astronomer Carl Sagan held the David Duncan Professorship of Astronomy and Space Studies at Cornell University. Endowed positions provide monetary benefits to their holders and are reserved for the most distinguished faculty.

Full professors achieve their rank after vigorous faculty and administrative review, which certifies the quality of their scholarship and research. Most noteworthy, promotion from associate professor to professor requires demonstrated competence in directing doctoral-level students. Thus, full professors have a track record for the guidance of Ph.D. students.

Associate professors are mid-level academicians who have generally been granted tenure. Tenure is a promissory arrangement. It implies confidence on the part of administration and faculty peers that the faculty member will continue to grow and contribute as a scholar and researcher for the period of time that he or she remains at the university. Tenure also guarantees that faculty may pursue their scholarly work without interference from internal and external forces. This is the nature of academic freedom.

Assistant professors are promoted to associate professors after a period of four to seven years. During the trial period, assistant professors must demonstrate research and teaching competencies, and their capabilities to serve the university through faculty committee work and other assignments. Accomplishments are evaluated by faculty and administration before tenure is granted. Most importantly, tenure and promotion to associate professor involves an up-or-out decision. If assistant professors are not promoted within a set period (usually six years), they lose their appointments.

Some graduate research departments have instructor-level faculty. These people usually hold Ph.D. degrees, or they may be close to completing their doctoral dissertations.

The teaching faculty is completed with graduate teaching assistants (TAs). TAs are typically hired part-time to help faculty with undergraduate lecture and laboratory courses. TA assignments are made by department chairs or deans and involve responsibilities to a professorial faculty member who is often not the TA's advisor.

Postdoctoral students, fellows, or researchers are usually full-time Ph.D.-level researchers who are supported by grants or contracts. These so-called "postdocs" report to individual faculty and generally have few other duties in a department or program.

Besides postdocs, graduate research departments often have full-time research staff. These people may have doctoral degrees and may conduct independent research. Thus, they may have a title such as research scientist, research assistant professor, or senior scientist. Research scientist–type individuals are rarely tenured, and they often support themselves through personally obtained grants and contracts.

Other full-time research staff include equipment maintenance people, shop workers (e.g., electrical shop, glassblowing shop), and technicians. Technicians are often baccalaureate-level professionals who perform research under the supervision of a Ph.D.-level staff or faculty member.

Graduate research departments and programs also have administrative and clerical staff. Purchasing, scheduling, and word processing are some of the many activities conducted by these important staff members. Frequently, these staff are overworked, underpaid, and unappreciated. They deserve the respect due all professionals.

Allegiances and Obligations

Professional development requires allegiances and commitments. Allegiance is owed to science and the pursuit of truth, and to one's university, department or program, and discipline, in that order. Students bear the mark of their university and their discipline or program—through publication, through résumés, and through contacts with friends and colleagues. After earning an advanced degree, students' names are tied to their programs or departments and advisors for life! These associations will be treasured most if good relationships are developed with faculty, staff, and colleagues. Faculty–graduate student relationships, in particular, are influenced by students' attitudes, commitments, and independent creative development. These topics are considered in the next chapter.

2 | ATTITUDES, COMMITMENTS, AND CREATIVITY

My life is what I have done, my scientific work; the one is inseparable from the other. The work is the expression of my inner development.

—C. G. Jung

Productive and rewarding scholarship and research do not come easily. They require unique personal traits and practices. Some characteristics must already be part of the individual; other personality features, including creativity, can be improved with experience.

Attitudes and Commitments

Research (discovery of new knowledge) and scholarship (creative organization, criticism, interpretation, and reinterpretation of facts and concepts), in and of themselves, can develop commitment. However, to become successful, graduate students must adopt a take-charge attitude and develop what can be referred to as skeptical optimism—asking tough questions and looking for alternatives and ways through problems. In other words, graduate students become successful through commitment and a desire to be creative and productive in research and scholarship.

Commitment involves an interesting feedback relationship. Reid noted, "It has been my experience that the most unattractive problem becomes absorbingly interesting when one digs into it . . . when you really get acquainted with a problem, you are apt to fall in love with it."[1] Students who achieve the results necessary to earn a degree and succeed professionally do so through extraordinary commitment. This commitment, in turn, "fuels" the creativity necessary for greater ac-

8

complishment. The Nobel Laureate geneticist Barbara McClintock noted, "I was just so interested in what I was doing I could hardly wait to get up in the morning and get at it. One of my friends, a geneticist, said I was a child, because only children can't wait to get up in the morning and get at it."[2] Richard Hoffman, a world-class biologist, noted, "I think that anybody who's going to make a contribution to science has got to be almost pathologically motivated. A person who is going to be good in science should be as dedicated as a person who's trying to make the Olympics."[3]

A number of practices and occurrences nurture commitment to research and scholarly efforts. Most importantly, highest priority must be given to research and scholarship. Throughout graduate school, there are great demands made on students' time. Courses must be taken, seminars attended, and other responsibilities (e.g., teaching assistantships) fulfilled. It is easy to get into the position of "not having enough time for research and scholarship," but research and scholarship are the most important activities in graduate education. Successful students or professionals do not find time for research (scholarship), they *make* time for research (scholarship). This is accomplished by reserving certain times each day and each week for research and scholarly activities. Stated differently, a day does not go by without some movement toward these goals. At first the necessary discipline may be developed by putting in a minimum amount of time, perhaps only 30 minutes to one hour per day. Within weeks or months, it will become difficult to spend so "little" time at research and scholarship—an investment has been made.

Research and scholarship often involve long-term projects that will require patience to see the projects through. It often helps to break larger problems into smaller ones and achieve the overall goal in parts. A companion to patience is thoroughness. The proof of a hypothesis must come from experiments that test many different possibilities. This may take much experimentation and data analysis.

Thoroughness is supported by continual summarization and careful documentation of results. A common temptation is to forget negative results and omit them from research notebooks or their equivalents. Another temptation is to delay inordinately the recording of research results. These are serious mistakes that can lead to needless repetition of unproductive experimentation.

Conducting research requires a certain level of emotional detachment that allows hypotheses to be challenged and possibly found wrong. Encourage this attitude by limiting speculation about results and admitting ignorance when appropriate. The latter is especially important when engaging in interdisciplinary research in which experiments are performed with unfamiliar methods.

Creativity

Creative scientists produce work that is original and is valued by others in the same field. For the beginning graduate student, these requirements are difficult because of the implied evaluation of published work, which may not appear until after the dissertation is written. There are, however, intervening evaluations of research by advisors and thesis committee members that help the creative development process.

Creative research and scholarship result in a novel idea or product. Newness alone, however, is not enough. For example, an agricultural scientist might find that precious-metal foils protect plants from certain damaging wavelengths of artificially produced sunlight. The cost restrictions of these findings limit their usefulness. Thus, for the applied scientist at least, the idea or product must be novel *and* useful—both criteria are necessary to secure a U.S. patent. In basic research, by contrast, the usefulness of discoveries may not be apparent for years.

In addition to novelty and usefulness, creative research and scholarship involve transformation and condensation. Jackson and Messick defined "transformation" as a property that alters the constraints of reality: a work that defies tradition and yields a new perspective, a work that forces us to "see" reality in a new way.[4] Rocha e Silva noted, "To *see* is to go deep into the meaning of a phenomenon. It is the attitude that leads to the creation of a new theory that may change one's outlook of the universe." The scientist who "sees" and believes in a new reality is, at the beginning, alone—mistrusted by colleagues and laypersons.[5]

A historically significant example of "transformation" is found in the theory of evolution. Darwin melded ideas from Malthusian economics with his own observations during a five-year journey on the *Beagle* (from 1831 to 1836)—especially the insights gained during his travels through the Galapagos Islands—to develop his thoughts on natural selection.[6]

The final necessary characteristic of creative research and scholarship, as noted earlier, is condensation. This is exemplified by works that encompass many ideas. Jackson and Messick noted that these works are "products [discoveries] that warrant close and repeated examination [and] . . . do not divulge their total meaning on first viewing. These products offer something new each time we experience them. . . . They have about them an intensity and concentration of meaning requiring continued contemplation."[4] The theory of evolution also represents a work that rates high in condensation because Darwin developed his explanation of the origins of animal life using a range of research efforts and discoveries that preceded him by at least 100 years.

People are frequently misled by the term "theory" as it is used in science and as it applies to a theory like evolution. The debate on teaching creationism or evolution in schools, for example, often focuses on the notion that evolution is just a theory that is not proved. Yet, scientific theories are never fully proved. Rather, they become more and more accepted as proofs develop. Eventually, theories are replaced by broader theories, and the process of proofs continues.

Levels of Creativity

The word "creativity" is used loosely in society. It tends to be confused with popularity, productivity, and professional visibility. Also, people may be called creative when they achieve modest goals such as winning first place in a high school essay contest or science fair. These individuals are better described as amateur creatives.

Donald Cram, a distinguished professor of chemistry at UCLA and advisor of graduate students for more than three decades, differentiates between operational and conceptual creativity.[7] In Cram's experience, almost all students are operationally creative, while "only about 5 to 10 percent . . . are conceptually creative. They are the ones that formulate research objectives. They not only know how to get things done, but they know what should be done." The transition from organizational to conceptual creativity is often signaled by researchers' descriptions of experimental results. The beginning researcher may comment about a failed experiment: "I tried that approach and it failed. What should I try next?" As experience is gained, an advisor may begin to hear: "I tried that approach and it failed, but I have some ideas for alternative approaches." With time, effort, and some guidance, the beginner integrates new approaches with new hypotheses—conceptual creativity emerges. And conceptually creative scientists or "auctors" (from the Latin, meaning maker, builder, author, or inventor), as noted by Mansfield and Busse, produce works that embody novelty, usefulness, transformation, and condensation.[8]

It might be asked: What traits and practices lead to conceptually creative or auctor-level work? Simultaneously it should be acknowledged that there are no quantum leaps in creativity, even for auctors. Rather, a continuum of creativity exists from amateur creatives to conceptually creative researchers and scholars.

There appear to be three preconditions for auctor-level scientific creativity: above-average intelligence, advanced education, and emotional balance. For graduate students, the first prerequisite is demonstrated through entrance requirements (i. e., grades and GRE scores) of graduate programs. The need for advanced education is evident, and the importance of commitment has been emphasized previously. Also, the specialization and depth of study required of graduate students takes time. Students should not feel discouraged if they seem initially to lack creative acumen. Often, creative insights barely start to develop during the last year or so of graduate study. Moreover, some scientists believe that creativity only starts to blossom after several years of research.

Roe proposed that a minimum level of emotional adjustment is necessary for creative research and scholarship.[9] Indeed, only the emotionally balanced individual will be able to develop the persistence and commitment that are needed for in-depth study. Some researchers also believe that persistence and commitment are related to the pleasure derived from being alone and from one's level of self-confidence.

Many students have the prerequisites for becoming an auctor-level creative scientist. To develop perspective, however, the traits of acknowledged creative scientists are reviewed below.

Characteristics of Auctors

MacKinnon[10] described six characteristics that are associated with creative scientists:

1. autonomy
2. personal flexibility and openness
3. need for originality
4. need for recognition
5. commitment to work
6. aesthetic sensitivities

Auctors are autonomous. They display independence and accept nothing on blind faith or the mere say-so of "authorities." Autonomy should be promoted in graduate programs, and it will be nurtured by good advisors and mentors (see Chapter 3). Indeed, a criterion for choosing an advisor is the advisor's reputation for fostering graduate student autonomy.

Creative scientists are flexible and open to new experience and interpretations. They are unconcerned with strict adherence to rules and regulations, and they reject dogmatic behavior. While a lack of dogmatism is critical, the researcher must adhere to some prescribed routines as they occur in experimental protocols (strict sets of directions for experiments as used often in animal and human subjects research). Also, successful creative scientists adopt a sense of professionalism in meeting deadlines and in dealing with support staff. These characteristics involve habits that should be reinforced during graduate education.

Flexibility and openness require the toleration of uncertainty and complexity. Creative scientists have faith that well-thought-out hypotheses, good experimental design, and persistence will lead to truth through research.

It requires courage to attempt new experimental routines and procedures. For the beginning graduate student, the fear of new methods or techniques can hamper progress in research. This is counteracted, in part, by choosing an advisor who helps overcome these apprehensions. For example, the establishment of a hierarchical structure in research groups provides role models for new graduate students and provides mechanisms for helping all students progress. A good advisor also helps students learn the difference between ideas and good ideas. This is indicated in part by the quality of the journals that have published work of the advisor's former students.

Auctors need to be original and novel. They consciously strive to achieve goals that bolster ego and enhance self-esteem. The prominent sociologist William Wilson noted the importance of his graduate program in enkindling an "arrogance of confidence that was necessary for me to overcome a very impoverished background."[11] The need for originality pertains to scholars in many fields. Thornton Wilder, the Pulitzer Prize–winning author of Our Town, once noted, "I erase as I go along . . . I look forward so much I have only an imperfect memory for the past. When your eyes are directed to the future, you have no hurt feelings over the praises or criticism of the moment—because, moment by moment, the present becomes the past. You have a sense of forever beginning your career, of trying to offer something new to interest the community."[12]

Wilder's conviction expresses a need for professional recognition that is also a prominent characteristic of creative researchers and scholars. This trait is exemplified by disputes scientists have over priority claims to research findings. In this connection, auctors are more likely to be assertive than humble, and they jealously guard their lifestyles.

From the earlier discussion, it may not be surprising to learn that auctors show high levels of commitment. Mansfield and Busse described several studies showing that creative scientists work longer and harder, and are more productive, than less creative peers.[8]

The talented biographer Evelyn Fox Keller noted, "Throughout history, artists and poets, lovers and mystics, have known and written about the 'knowing' that comes from the loss of self—from the state of subjective fusion with the object of knowledge. Scientists have known it, too. Einstein once wrote: 'The state of feeling which makes one capable of such achievements is akin to that of the religious worshipper or of one who is in love.'"[2] The commitment necessary to achieve this level of dedication should begin in graduate school.

It has been noted by MacKinnon[10] and Zuckerman[13] that auctor-level researchers experience aesthetic satisfaction from their work. Creative researchers find beauty in science and in solutions to problems. Their commitment is fostered by gratification experienced after proving hypotheses through personally designed and conducted (or directed) experimentation. Shortly before his death, Richard Feynman, Nobel Laureate in physics, spoke fondly of the psychic satisfaction derived from some of his more important research: "I went on to work out the equations on wobbles. . . . I was 'playing'—working, really—with some old problem that I loved so much, that I had stopped working on when I went to Los Alamos: my thesis-type problem; all those old-fashioned, wonderful things. . . . There was no importance to what I was doing, but ultimately there was. The diagrams and the whole business that I got the Nobel Prize for came from the piddling around with the wobbling plate."[14] The intriguing link between fond remembrance and work on a "thesis-type problem" will be considered again in later chapters.

In summary, auctor-level scientists need to be original and seek professional recognition. They are committed to their work, and they display flexibility and openness to experience; they act autonomously and find beauty in their work. This montage serves as a model and as the basis of a plan for self-determined improvement.

The plan will be influenced by conscious choices and to some degree by chance. Four types of chance relevant to graduate research have been described by Austin.[15] Blind luck (Chance I) is independent of personal characteristics and functions in everyone's life. Chance II, or good luck, results from general exploratory behavior. The more one reads, experiments, and practices introspection, the greater the possibility that random ideas will occur in certain juxtaposition to spark creative discovery.

Chance III is associated with serendipity and with Pasteur's assertion that chance favors the prepared mind. This type of luck occurs with experience and requires a degree of courage to face the initially inexplicable result. Experienced investigators know that research frequently involves pursuit of unusual data points. Many important discoveries were, initially, findings that were at odds with expected findings. The "unprepared mind" has the tendency to discard such results and begin again, thinking that the experiment went wrong. The more experienced researcher, however, will meet the serendipitous challenge by performing additional experimentation and by modifying hypotheses as necessary.

Chance IV provides useful ideas through individualized action. Business professionals choose sports activities such as golf because of the advantageous contacts that are made during play. Hobbies or leisure time activities can be chosen to complement scientific work. For example, graduate students in aerospace engineering could reinforce their research pursuits by having an interest in astronomy. Marine biology students might take up scuba diving. This can be referred to as "making things count double."

The development of auctor-level scientists is dependent on choices made throughout a graduate career. Some of these choices will be required during the first few months of graduate school and are considered in the next chapter.

References

[1] E. E. Reid, *Invitation to Chemical Research* (Palisades, NJ: Franklin, 1961).

[2] E. F. Keller, *A Feeling for the Organism* (New York: Freeman, 1983).

[3] K. McDonald, What has up to 752 feet and could prove that continents drift? The millipede, says a Radford U. professor who has spent 35 years studying the animal, *The Chronicle of Higher Education* 33 (No. 5) (1981), pp. 5–6.

[4] P. W. Jackson and S. Messick, The person, the product, and the response: Conceptual problems in the assessment of creativity. In *Creativity and Learning*, J. Kagan, ed. (Boston: Houghton Mifflin, 1967), pp. 1–19.

[5] M. Rocha e Silva, *The Rational Frontiers of Science* (Malabar, FL: Krieger, 1982).

[6] R. Weisberg, The myth of scientific creativity. In *Windows on Creativity and Invention*, J. G. Richardson, ed. (Mount Airey, MD: Lomond, 1988), pp. 39–61.

[7] D. Cram, Tribe and leader, *Council of Graduate Schools Communicator* 32 (No. 4) (1989), p. 1.

[8] R. S. Mansfield and T. V. Busse, *The Psychology of Creativity and Discovery: Scientists and Their Work* (Chicago: Nelson-Hall, 1981).

[9] A. Roe, A psychological study of eminent biologists, *Psychology Monograph* 65 (No. 331) (1951).

[10] D. W. MacKinnon, The nature and nurture of creative talent, *American Psychologist* 17 (1962), pp. 484–95.

[11] P. L. Dion, An interview with Dr. William Julius Wilson, *Graduate and Professional Student News* (Washington State University), (October 1988), p. 5.

[12] Thornton Wilder, author dies, *Austin American Statesman* 62 (No. 134) (1975), p. 20.

[13] H. A. Zuckerman, *Scientific Elite: Nobel Laureates in the United States* (New York: Free Press, 1977).

[14] R. P. Feynman, *"Surely You're Joking Mr. Feynman!" Adventures of a Curious Character* (New York: Norton, 1985).

[15] J. H. Austin, *Chase, Chance, and Creativity: The Lucky Art of Novelty* (New York: Columbia University Press, 1978).

3 | MAKING CHOICES

*All I have learnt of any value has been
self-taught.*

—Charles Darwin

Plans for becoming a creative researcher and scholar involve choices. The type of research chosen, the choice of research advisor or other role models and support, the selection of a research problem and the proper tools to solve it, and the choice of thesis and dissertation committee members all involve thoughtful decisions.

Types of Research

Research is often subdivided into two types—basic and applied. Basic research involves study of the fundamental properties of subjects and their behavior. Applied research focuses on the usefulness of subjects and their behavior. "Subjects" is used broadly to include materials, animals, and human beings. To paraphrase Renan,[1] basic research helps us to seek truth; applied research serves our material well-being.

Basic research is sometimes maligned because of the perceived unimportance of specific projects. Former U.S. Senator William Proxmire was known for his so-called Golden Fleece awards, which were issued periodically for government-sponsored projects thought to be silly or useless.[2] Some of these awards went to basic biomedical and social-behavioral research efforts. Yet, the apparently useless basic research of today may serve as a necessary precursor to vital applied research of tomorrow. The key factor is the quality of the research and whether the research addresses fundamental questions about subjects and phenomena. Both basic and applied research are essential, and the choice of one or the other should not be influenced by prejudices. The choice of basic or applied research should also be based on personal preferences and needs.

Basic research requires a dedication to narrow purposes. This is compatible with individuals who enjoy isolation and who relish the idea of becoming world experts in a limited area. Basic researchers work at the frontier. Equipment and other experimental tools necessary to solve problems may not be available commercially. In the physical sciences, for example, equipment may have to be constructed; algorithms may have to be developed. These challenges require aptitude for mechanical, electronic, mathematical, and computer-science skills. Applied researchers, on the other hand, will generally be able to use commercially available electronic and computer-based equipment, perhaps with minor modifications.

An applied researcher engages in projects that may offer immediate benefit to society. Consequently, this type of research could fulfill an inner need to help people. During their careers, applied researchers are likely to interact with greater numbers of people than their colleagues in basic research. Also, applied researchers may have greater opportunities for professional consulting and for the development of combination career goals such as teacher-scientist, manager-scientist, or consultant-scientist.

Applied research is more likely to provide quick results than its basic counterpart. The psychic rewards of basic research, however, may be greater than those of applied research. The choice of basic or applied research should therefore be made according to personal and professional preferences and the recognition that research, from basic to applied, lies on a continuum. Notable basic researchers often perceive useful ends to their research; effective applied researchers frequently incorporate basic research approaches in solving even the most applied problems.

Choosing an Advisor and Mentor

Advisors have a powerful influence on graduate students' development as scientists. Thus, it is important to assess the advantages of different types of advisors and to find an advisor who supports creative development and who interacts well with people.

The best advisors are those who are most adept at assisting the transition from student to colleague. These talents are often categorized under the term "mentor," or someone who is dedicated to the holistic (intellectual, professional, and personal) development of graduate students. Hereafter, the word "advisor" is intended to reflect advisors who are also mentors.

For women and students from underrepresented groups, it is especially important to find advisors who have an understanding of professional development needs. Women compete well with men in mathematics and science in high school, undergraduate programs, and entrance into graduate programs.[3-4] However, in graduate school a greater proportion of women drop out. Some authors point to a "chilly climate" for women in graduate programs, caused primarily by unsympathetic advisors and graduate student colleagues. Parallel problems may be faced by students from underrepresented groups. Sheila E. Widnall, the Abby Rockefeller Mauze Professor of Aeronautics and Astronautics at MIT, asserts that these problems are due in large measure to advisors' inattention to the development of students' self-esteem.[4] Specifically, the independent nature of graduate education can handicap underrepresented students (which includes women in some science-based fields, especially the physical sciences) if expectations are not carefully described and reinforced. Standards must not be lowered, but advisors should be found who make all students feel welcome in research groups. Widnall noted correctly, "The adviser is the primary gatekeeper for the professional self-esteem of the student, the rate of progress toward the degree, and access to future opportunities."[4] All students should choose an advisor wisely.

Advisors vary in their supervisory skills, experience, and obligations to the university. Good advisors can be found among all ranks and ages. However, supervisory approaches vary, which allows categorization of three types of advisors: (1) the collaborator type, (2) the hands-off type, and (3) the senior scientist type.

Collaborator types are typically young academically (i.e., assistant professors) and are keen to have their students achieve quick results. These advisors generally have more time for research because of light service responsibilities. In the laboratory-based fields, this means that collaborators work side by side with students at the bench. In social-behavioral areas, the collaborator will assist with data collection and analysis. Collaborator advisors have a vested interest in their students' research results. In some disciplines, this means joint publications. In other fields, the collaborator advisor merely receives credit for advising students who complete degree requirements. Regardless of the field, publications and graduate students are of vital importance to this advisor, who may be seeking promotion and tenure. Because of the need for productivity, the collaborator advisor may bias choices of research problems. The need for results may cause this advisor to encourage students to tackle problems of low risk and low significance.

The hands-off advisor is generally at midlevel academically and is likely to have administrative or other service responsibilities. These advisors have less time to spend on projects directly, but they may be less "greedy" for results. This is a two-sided issue. The hands-off advisor may allow excessive time to complete work. On the other hand, hands-off advisors may be sources of wise counsel, and they will encourage pursuit of problems of comparatively higher risk and significance.

Senior scientist advisors are well-established faculty. These advisors have varying amounts of time to spend with students. The quality of attention, however, may be the best of all because of their extensive past experience. If a senior advisor is an outstanding researcher in her or his field, a desirable master scientist–student relationship may ensue. Mansfield and Busse noted, for example, that more than half the American Nobel Prize winners before 1981 worked under Nobel Laureates of earlier generations.[5] In some instances, however, senior scientist advisors are living on past glories and may have become obsolete in their fields. Working with these individuals can lead to minor research problems and to the unfortunate possibility of being trained in outdated methods.

All types of advisors will display various professional and personal characteristics. Of prime importance is the advisor's reputation as a scientist. This can be judged by his or her curriculum vitae, which can be obtained either before or during a personal interview. Determine how many papers the prospective advisor has published in high-quality journals. Select a number of the apparently important citations and check them through *Science Citation Index*. This provides an indication of how often the advisor's work is cited by others, which is a measure of its importance.

Determine how many invited presentations and consultantships the prospective advisor has had during the past five years. Check to see how many grants this advisor has successfully completed during her or his career. Make inquiries about the reputation of the prospective advisor as a teacher. It is also important to see how many students have graduated under the advisor's direction. Try to determine the current position and rank of former students. All of these factors are measures of the prospective advisor's stature.

In a field involving laboratory research, ask to see the prospective advisors' laboratories in operation. Visit with graduate students working in these laboratories. Note the number of professionals managed by the advisors. A research group of more than 10 individuals, including graduate students, postdoctoral fellows, and technicians, is unwieldy except for the most talented academic managers.

Ask about the organizational structure of the laboratory. Are there hierarchical systems for helping graduate students who are new members of the group? For example, many advisors have a "big sibling" system in which novices receive day-to-day training from a senior graduate student or postdoctoral fellow for several months to a year. Other systems may have been developed to help newcomers achieve sufficient training to permit independent experimentation. Find out if these systems have existed for some time and if they seem to function well. Make sure the advisor has grant funds to cover research costs. This is of vital importance since few departments have sufficient intramural funds to support outstanding research, particularly in laboratory-based research.

Choose an advisor who is demanding. The best advisors are those who require periodic reports, meet regularly with students both individually and collectively, and expect a high level of performance but supervise with caring and compassion. Indeed, as noted earlier, the best advisor transcends the strict "advisor" role to become a mentor, the "peer-to-be—one who stimulates and supports independent development—one who encourages a rapid transition from graduate student to colleague through insightful guidance, trust, and mutual respect."[6] For most students, therefore, the choice of an advisor will be one who will also serve as mentor.

Effective advisors promote the traits of auctors that were discussed in Chapter 2. Of particular importance are the following: (1) respect for individuality, (2) enthusiasm and personal support, (3) patience, and (4) recognition. Does the prospective advisor respect student contributions? Does the advisor have a record of encouraging students to contribute ideas and judgments in joint research efforts? How enthusiastic is the prospective advisor about previous students' achievements? Does the prospective advisor have a history of patience with students and their developmental problems? One measure of this is prior success in directing students as indicated in part by student turnover. Have students who studied under this advisor graduated regularly and in a timely fashion during the past five years? Does the advisor have a record of losing students?

What kind of recognition has the prospective advisor given to students in the past? Has she or he arranged for students to present papers at scientific meetings? In joint research in which the student's efforts were paramount, does the student's name appear first on resultant publications?

During a personal interview with the prospective advisor, engage in conversation that will answer the questions raised in the above paragraphs. If the advisor seems vague or evasive on points raised, he or she may have deficiencies. After talking, ask to visit with some of his or her current students. The resulting discussions must be done tactfully and cautiously because you may become privy to hearsay information.

One method for choosing an advisor is to work with a potential advisor on a trial basis for a semester. This is the best way to evaluate the advisor's management style and compatibility. The trial period may be mandated by departmental policy. In some departments, students are expected to rotate among two or three faculty members before choosing an advisor.

Having a university fellowship or teaching assistantship may provide the advantage of being in the department for one to six months before having to choose an advisor. This situation provides the necessary time for an evaluation.

In summary, the choice of an advisor should be based on the prospective advisor's

- accomplishments in teaching and research
- enthusiasm for advising students
- experience in directing graduate students
- management and organization of his or her research group
- reputation for setting high standards in a congenial atmosphere
- compatible personality
- ability to serve as a mentor

Despite all efforts, an incompatible advisor may be chosen. Problems can sometimes be worked out through honest communication. If not, it is important to change advisors. Most advisors have experienced changes in students' preferences, and they are not as shocked by changes as some students might imagine. If difficulties occur during the transition, help should be sought from a graduate coordinator, department chair, and graduate school dean, in that order.

Role Models

It is useful to adopt role models. These should consist of departmental or program faculty and graduate students, as well as other researchers. For women or underrepresented students, it may be necessary to look to campuswide organizations (e.g., association of faculty women, graduate and professional student organizations, multicultural student center) for suitable role models. The faculty and researcher role models should have talents complementary to those of an advisor. Graduate student role models should be representative of the different stages of one's graduate career (e.g., first-year students and students already admitted to candidacy).

Financial Support

Graduate students are supported in one of three ways: (1) teaching assistantship, (2) research assistantship, or (3) research fellowship. Typical teaching assistantships are half-time appointments that include a 20-hour commitment per week to teaching in one's own or a related department. The teaching responsibilities may range from grading papers to teaching in one or more courses. Before accepting a teaching assistantship, find out what specific duties are required. Some departments are more flexible than others with time commitments.

If you choose to become a teaching assistant (TA), it will be advantageous to seek guidance on the art of teaching. Many universities have courses specifically designed for beginning TAs. Look for offerings that consider issues such as

- the culture of the American classroom, including civil rights issues related to gender, race, ethnic origin, and sexual orientation
- modern theories of learning
- characteristics of good teachers
- techniques for involving students in learning
- using audiovisual tools including multimedia
- use of the World Wide Web (www) in teaching
- evaluating and grading students
- university policies regarding teaching
- ethics and teaching

It will also be helpful to read one or two books on the art of teaching. Two books recommended by consummate teachers are those by Bonwell and Elson,[7] and McKeachie.[8]

Research assistantships, like teaching assistantships, typically involve half-time appointments. Research assistantships are developed through grant funds and require commitment to a specific project. The grant holder or principal investigator may or may not be your advisor. By working for an advisor, it may be possible to dovetail the responsibilities of a research assistantship with the objectives of thesis or dissertation research. Alternatively, research may be performed that is unrelated to research necessary for a thesis or dissertation. Choosing a research assistantship supervisor is like selecting an advisor. In addition, the nature of the project is important, along with its compatibility with research and career goals.

Research fellowships involve support with no expectation that specific tasks will be performed. This type of support is ideal because it permits complete devotion to thesis or dissertation research and course work. The level of support is usually similar to that available through assistantships.

Income tax liabilities on assistantship and fellowship stipends and tuition waivers have varied during the past several years. Departmental and graduate school administrative offices should be consulted for current regulations before presuming the tax status of any of these sources of support.

Programs of Study

Some departments develop rigid policy on programs of study for graduate degrees. Other units may have looser approaches to graduate education. Ideally, a program of study should be flexible yet provide core knowledge needed for performance as a researcher.

For many Ph.D. degree programs different plans can be envisioned for completion of course work and research. Some plans may stress the integration of research throughout one's graduate career. Others may call for block efforts, first in course work and then in research. Adoption of the integrated approach requires early research activities that may not be possible in all fields. The integrated plan, however, emphasizes the importance of research in graduate training, which was proposed earlier. Also, the integrated plan requires careful time management. Development of this skill in graduate school will be beneficial in a subsequent career.

A disadvantage of the integrated plan is that course work necessary to pursue certain aspects of research may not be completed in a timely fashion. This is a major advantage of the block-effort plan.

Also, graduate students may be attracted to the block-effort plan because it seems less risky than an integrated effort. It can be comforting to think, "When I have developed all the tools necessary to do my research, then I will start." This is somewhat naive because research stimulates and reinforces learning. Indeed, material learned from experimental work will be retained better and with greater understanding than that gained strictly through course work.

The integrated and block-effort plans involve compromises. Some permutation of these plans should be developed to meet the demands of the discipline and an advisor. For example, some graduate courses involve mini-research projects. Other courses may have requirements such as the preparation of research proposals which lead to ideas for thesis or dissertation projects. These are examples of making things count double.

Regardless of choices of courses and research, it is desirable to have a written plan of study. The plan should be developed and approved by your advisor, thesis or dissertation committee, and the graduate school.

Interdisciplinary versus Disciplinary Research

University faculties and departments are organized along disciplinary lines. Most faculty are devoted to research that advances their fields, and, by definition, work in a discipline is narrowly focused. Disciplinary work is a useful starting point for graduate students. During advancement, however, an awareness must be developed of the interdisciplinary nature of problems facing scientists and society. Many of these problems call for interdisciplinary research, which involves the joint, coordinated, and continuously integrated research efforts of investigators from different disciplinary backgrounds. Interdisciplinary researchers cross traditional disciplinary boundaries and work so closely with one another that individual contributions become difficult to identify. In chemical-biological interdisciplinary studies, for example, the chemist will perform biological experiments and the biologist will do chemical work. The exchange of roles prompts new ideas and leads to deeper understanding, greater expertise, and more rapid solutions to problems. This mixing and blending of research activities may also lead to the development of new fields or "disciplines." For example, the relatively "new" field of computer science has roots in mathematics, engineering, and linguistics.

Progressive academicians and scientists appreciate the value of interdisciplinary research efforts. An executive director of agricultural biotechnology with the Ciba-Geigy Corporation, Mary-Dell Chilton, noted: "Interdisciplinary, interdepartmental, collaborative research, which has rarely been tolerated, encouraged, or rewarded in academia, can make unexpected large changes in our intellectual landscape. It may even lead to practical applications. Breakthroughs most often occur at the edges of two or more traditional disciplines. It is important that we place proper value on interdisciplinary research and researchers."[9]

In 1995, the Committee on Science, Engineering, and Public Policy (fondly referred to as COSEPUP) of the National Research Council (NRC)[10] issued a report that contained the recommendation that graduate students be educated and trained more broadly and that opportunities be developed for interdisciplinary research.[11]

Chilton's and the COSEPUP position should not be misconstrued. Interdisciplinary research is no substitute for good disciplinary training during the greater part of a graduate career. It is advisable, however, to seek exposure to interdisciplinary activities in graduate as well as postdoctoral training, since most researchers engage in interdisciplinary research during their professional careers.

Research Problem

Following are points to consider when choosing a research problem:

1. Can it be enthusiastically pursued?
2. Can interest be sustained by it?
3. Is the problem solvable?
4. Is it worth doing?
5. Will it lead to other research problems?
6. Is it manageable in size?
7. What is its potential for making original contributions to the literature?
8. If the problem is solved, will it be reviewed well by scholars in your field?
9. Are you, or will you become, competent to solve it?
10. By solving it, will you have demonstrated independent skills in your discipline?
11. Will the necessary research prepare you in an area of demand or promise for the future?

The choice of a research problem should be a highly personalized decision. It may involve background, interests, perceived research strengths, aesthetic judgments, and personal commitments. Some students in the biomedical sciences choose research related to a disease that afflicted a relative or close friend. Students in the social-behavioral sciences may feel deeply about a particular social injustice or condition. These "biases" can actually become the foundation for commitments that will last for years, or a lifetime.

Another important basis for the choice of a research problem can be the professional opportunities it leads to after graduation. It has been predicted that the following scientific areas will be of greatest commercial exploitation through the year 2000 and beyond:[12–15]

- Biotechnology—bioprocessing and production of pharmaceutical products including protein hormones, vaccines, and immunologically important substances; genetic engineering and recombinant DNA technology; production of industrial chemicals and microelectronic memory; production of plants and animals with unique properties including extraordinary production characteristics or resistance to disease and adverse environmental conditions
- Energy technology—alternative sources of energy including oxygenated solvent-modified petroleum products; catalysis; emission-control technology; energy-conversion technologies such as fuel and solar photoelectrochemical cells; recycling technology; renewable resources including hybrid woody plants
- Health and medical technology—combination organic and electronic systems for the diagnosis and treatment of illnesses; drug design through computer visualization, analysis, and molecular engineering; drugs that alter brain function and repair, memory, and consciousness; gene therapy; magnetic and other imaging systems such as positron-emission tomography; novel drug delivery systems; prostheses and other medical devices; tissue culture and other products and systems for the diagnosis of disease and toxicological conditions; xenographic transplantation
- Industrial technology—artificial intelligence and expert systems in manufacturing, energy prospecting, automotive diagnostics, medicine, insurance underwriting, and law enforcement; artificial vision and machine sensing of touch, force, and torque; automated manufacture of plastic films and coatings; food processing including nonthermal preservation; hazardous waste cleanup and remediation; nanofabrication technology; robotics and machine-human interactions

- Information technology—analog/digital integrated circuits, data storage and retrieval, electronic packaging, fiber optics, microelectronics, and microprocessor chips; geographic information and positioning systems for global atmospheric monitoring, environmental analysis, sustainable agriculture, and weather forecasting; software for virtual education, entertainment, medical, and industrial applications; telecommunications
- New materials and their applications—biomimetic and composite materials; ceramic and other superconducting materials; conductors and engines; smart (responsive to changes in environmental conditions) and superplastic materials; synthetic membranes

These industrial and scientific developments will require analytical chemists, biochemists, biomedical engineers, chemical engineers, chemical physicists, civil engineers, computer scientists, electrical and computer engineers, environmental engineers and scientists, geologists, mathematicians, mechanical engineers, medicinal chemists, microbiologists, molecular biologists, neuroscientists, organic chemists, pharmaceutics specialists, pharmacologists, physicists, physiologists, physical chemists, polymer scientists, psychologists, radiation biologists, and toxicologists with state-of-the-art training. Furthermore, there will be needs for new types of scientists—ones who can combine fields such as computer science or mathematics with biochemistry (i.e., to solve biotechnological problems), and chemical physics with materials engineering (i.e., to tackle advanced materials design and analysis).

The choice of a research problem may be dictated in part by an already-funded research project. In such a case, objectives have to be meshed with those in the grant proposal. Some lack of enthusiasm for the project at first may be replaced by intensified interest when the project evolves, as indicated earlier.

As noted by Medawar, solvable problems are those involving hypotheses that can be tested by practical experiments.[16] Worthy research problems are also fundable and lead to many other problems. Indeed, one of the most commonly asked questions at dissertation orals is something like, "If you could stay a few more years, what problems would you pursue as uncovered by your dissertation research?" Such a question contains an element of irony for the candidate who typically cannot conceive of spending any more time on campus. Yet, this candidate may extend the doctoral research, especially if she or he goes on to an academic career. Some academicians have misgivings about this prospect. Nevertheless, the choice of a research problem that is fundable and leads to other problems can be of immense benefit later.

A research problem must be solvable in a reasonable time period, have the right balance of breadth and focus, and must have potential for contributions to the literature. The latter objective is met if the problem does one or more of the following:[17-18]

- Uncovers new facts
- Suggests new relationships
- Challenges currently accepted truths and assumptions
- Provides new insights into poorly understood phenomena
- Stimulates collaboration and cooperation with colleagues

If it meets two or more of these objectives, the resulting work should be regarded highly by others, including the members of a thesis or dissertation committee. By solving a challenging and significant problem, skills will have been demonstrated that should certify competence in a discipline.

Courses and Research Aids

Courses are chosen on the basis of core curricula requirements or disciplinary objectives in the plan of study. Courses that provide tools of research should also be considered (e.g., computer sciences, statistics, technical writing), along with courses that provide opportunities for research orientation and professional development. A beginning graduate seminar in the School of Fisheries at the University of Washington, for example, uses topics in this book as well as specialized readings and presentations in modern fisheries science to serve the latter purposes.

Besides university sources, various professional societies and commercial publishers have developed CD-ROM, film, software, slide-tape, and videotape materials that are useful adjuncts to formally organized course work. For example, the American Chemical Society (ACS) has produced audio and video courses with diverse titles such as "Applied Problem Solving Through Creative Thinking," "Computer-Aided Genetic and Protein Engineering," "Fundamentals of Experimental Design," and "Technical Writing."[19] The ACS also offers a Satellite TV Seminar Series with program titles such as "Conversations with Nobel Laureates in Chemistry" and "Teaching Chemistry."[20]

International Business Machines (IBM), through its "Global Campus," offers computer-based communications and people-skills courses with titles such as "Manage Your Time Effectively," "Succeeding with Your Presentation: Prepare It, Deliver It," and "Team Building."[21]

The *Media Review Digest* (MRD)[22] describes all types of media. This guide also includes overall quality ratings based on editorial reviews. Other guides to audiovisual materials and software are available,[23-24] including a listing of materials[23] that can be ordered free of charge through a university library.

Several WWW resources are also available, including the American Association for the Advancement of Science Nextwave site (billed as "An Electronic Network for the Next Generation of Scientists")[25] and the American Physical Society's "Graduate Student Packet,"[26] just to name two.

Competency in foreign languages used to be a common requirement of doctoral programs. Many universities now permit substitution of tools of research (e.g., statistics, computer science) for language requirements. Yet, knowledge of foreign languages may be important to students' career goals, especially as we move more toward a global society. Social-behavioral scientists such as sociologists and social psychologists should consider developing a reading and speaking knowledge of Spanish because of the rapidly growing Latino-Hispanic communities in many parts of the world. History-of-science scholars should plan studies of German and French. Physical- and engineering-science students might benefit from learning Japanese.

In general, the use of languages other than English has diminished in importance in science during the latter part of this century. Most journals publish articles in English, and international meetings rarely exclude presentations in English. The vast majority of resources available through the Internet and the WWW are in English. Knowledge of foreign languages, however, facilitates international collaborative efforts that are common among scientists. Such collaboration will become of increasing importance. Accordingly, all of the above factors should be weighed when deciding on foreign language study.

Thesis and Dissertation Committee Members

Masters' theses and doctoral dissertations are typically supervised by committees consisting of the following numbers of faculty members: M.S., three to four; Ph.D., three to six. An advisor chairs the committee, which is usually appointed through the graduate school one to three years before the degree is awarded.

Students often have input in the selection of their committee members. Thus, it is useful to begin early to note potential candidates. Faculty who are young academically are often very helpful during thesis and dissertation work because of their lighter commitments. They may also be the most demanding. The guidelines suggested for choosing an advisor are also valuable in selecting dissertation and thesis committee members.

Sometimes research problems involve a significant component from an allied field. A physical chemistry graduate student, for example, may have to construct an electronic apparatus to test and collect data on molten metal mixtures. A faculty member from electrical engineering would be a valuable asset on the student's committee. In an analogous situation, a genetics student may require complex statistical analyses for studies of mutations in *Drosophila* species. This student would be well advised to seek out a member of a statistics faculty for service on her or his committee.

Graduate work involves numerous choices. Many of these have been discussed above. One of the most important choices, however, involves the use of time, which is considered in the next chapter.

References

[1] P. Lacomte du Noüy, *Between Knowing and Believing* (New York: David McKay, 1967).

[2] W. Proxmire, *The Fleecing of America* (Boston: Houghton Mifflin, 1980).

[3] D. E. Koshland, Jr., Women in science, *Science* 239 (1988), p. 1473.

[4] S. E. Widnall, AAAS presidential lecture: Voices from the pipeline, *Science* 241 (1988), pp. 1740–45.

[5] R. S. Mansfield and T. V. Busse, *The Psychology of Creativity and Discovery: Scientists and Their Work* (Chicago: Nelson-Hall, 1981).

[6] C. Wiser, K. DePauw, and R. V. Smith, Graduate student mentoring: Is it important? *WSU Week* 6 (26) (1995), p. 4.

[7] C. C. Bonwell and J. A. Elson, *Active Learning: Creating Excitement in the Classroom* (Washington, D.C.: George Washington University, 1991).

[8] W. J. McKeachie, *Teaching Tips: Strategies, Research, and Theory for College and University Teachers*, 9th ed. (Lexington, MA: D. C. Heath, 1994).

[9] Mary-Dell Chilton, Casting bread upon the waters, *New Mexico State University Centennial Publication* (Las Cruces: New Mexico State University, 1988), pp. 37–45.

[10] The National Research Council is composed of the National Academy of Sciences, the National Academy of Engineering, and the Institute of Medicine.

[11] Committee on Science, Engineering, and Public Policy, *Reshaping the Graduate Education of Scientists and Engineers* (Washington, D.C.: National Academy Press, 1995). See also http://www.nap.edu/readingroom/books/grad/index.html

[12] W. F. Miller and P. E. Shay, *High Technology: Management and Policy Implications and Emerging Opportunities* (Palo Alto, CA: Stanford Research Institute, 1982).

[13] K. Eric Drexler, *Engines of Creation* (New York: Anchor Press, Doubleday, 1986).

[14] M. J. Cetron, W. Rocha, and R. Luckins, Long-term trends affecting the United States, *The Futurist* 22 (4) (1988), pp. 29–40.

[15] *Critical Technologies: The Role of Chemistry and Chemical Engineering* (Washington, D.C.: National Academy Press, 1992).

[16] P. B. Medawar, *Advice to a Young Scientist* (New York: Harper and Row, 1979).

[17] D. Madsen, *Successful Dissertations and Theses* (San Francisco: Jossey-Bass, 1983).

[18] Committee on Science, Engineering, and Public Policy, *Careers in Science and Engineering: A Student Planning Guide to Grad School and Beyond* (Washington, D.C.: National Academy Press, 1995). See also http://www.nap.edu/readingroom/books/careers/

[19] *Video Catalog (Video and Audio Products for Chemistry Educators, Researchers, and Students)* Number 3 (Washington, D.C.: American Chemical Society, 1996); Internet edition: http://www.acs.org/edugen2/education/conted/catalog/catlgtoc.html

[20] Satellite TV Seminar Series, Internet edition: http://www.acs.org/edugen2/education/conted/about_tv.htm

[21] Distance Learning Courses from IBM: http://www.europe.ibm.com/learningtechnology/section2/catalog/maincat.htm

[22] C. E. Wall, ed., *Media Review Digest*, 26th ed. (Ann Arbor, MI: Pierian Press, 1996).

[23] *Educational Film-Video Locator*, 2 vols., 4th ed. (New York: Bowker, 1989).

[24] *Educators Guide to Free Audio and Video Materials*, 39th ed. (Randolph, WI: Educators Progress Service, 1992).

[25] American Association for the Advancement of Science Nextwave www site: http://www.nextwave.org/

[26] The American Physical Society's "Graduate Student Packet" www site: http://aps.org/graduate/

4 | TIME MANAGEMENT

In human affairs the logical future,
determined by past and present conditions,
is less important than the willed future,
which is largely brought about by deliberate
choices.

—René Dubos

Time is asymmetric. It moves inexorably forward—it waits for no one. Effective use of time requires planning, as well as methods for organizing and executing plans.

Planning

Everyone has goals. Many people, however, do not reach their goals for lack of planning. Three sets of goals should be developed: lifetime, intermediate, and short-term.[1]

Lifetime goals should be written out. These goals should be lucid and measurable. For example, the goal of winning a major research prize is clear and measurable. In contrast, the goal of appreciating research in an allied field is fuzzy and unmeasurable. Other lifetime goals might include being elected to a departmental chair position at a major state university, successfully competing for a grant from the National Science Foundation, and securing a consultantship with a Fortune 500 corporation. A list of lifetime goals should be reviewed periodically.

Intermediate goals relate to outcomes anticipated during the next few years. For the beginning doctoral student, intermediate goals may include completing course work, preparing a doctoral research proposal, and achieving candidacy. Like lifetime goals, these are measurable and clearly stated.

Short-term goals involve outcomes expected during the next 12 months. These goals are more performance oriented (thus, some people would call them objectives), and they help with the achievement of intermediate goals. Examples of short-term goals are earning an A in a course, learning how to use computer software, and performing an experiment.

A list of intermediate and short-term goals becomes a To Do List. Items on one's To Do List should be classified by priority—for example, with letters A, B, and C.[1] Following are characteristics of these priorities.

Priority A

1. Critical
2. May be unpleasant to do
3. Goal related
4. Must be done today

Priority B

1. Important
2. Goal related
3. Must be done soon, but not today

Priority C

1. Can wait
2. May or may not be goal related
3. No significant time pressure
4. Usually easy, quick, and pleasant

After scanning this list, you may properly have concluded that A's are the most difficult, but highest priority, items. Similarly, Lakein[1] stated that 80 percent of one's goals are achieved by completing 20 percent of the most important items on a To Do List—the A's.

Despite the importance of A-priority items, C's can be very tempting. The latter are easy to accomplish, take little time, and involve the pleasure of completing something that can be crossed off the To Do List. Ways should be found to resist this temptation. B-priority items are important and become A's with time. Planning itself is never less than a B-priority item.

A transition from B to A can be represented by a paper that may be due in a core course taken during a fall term. A December 15 deadline may be known during the first week in September. The paper may be a B-priority item on the To Do List in September and October. As November approaches, the paper becomes an A-priority item.

The timing for this type of transition has to be customized. Dealing with A and B items in this way, however, creates reminders of impending deadlines. It also forces planning.

C-priority items rarely become A's and can often be avoided. One way of doing this is to have a drawer or box where C-related materials are tossed.[1] On occasion these C items might be reviewed and many discarded. Examples of C activities are reading advertisements for books and taking elective courses. C activities are often "nice to do," but they are not necessary to achieve important goals.

The continual pursuit of A-items can be encouraged by using a Daily To Do List prepared at the end of each previous working day. This separate To Do List may be a small, lined pad or computer document that is broken into two sections: Things To Do and Follow-Up. The pad or computer document is dated at the top and A items are listed in priority order: A-1, A-2, A-3, etc. These A-priority items might include turning in a report that is due, completing a necessary experiment, and attending a scheduled meeting with an advisor. Follow-up items are holdovers from the previous day. Each day, an attempt should be made to accomplish everything on the Daily To Do List.

Like a Daily To Do List, all papers handled should be dated. The dates become subtle reminders of work left undone or of impending deadlines.

Organization

The development of goals and the use of To Do Lists are essential for the organization of research and scholarly work. Of similar importance is the daily routine. There are times during the day when we are most alert and creative. For some, this may be from seven to nine in the morning; others work best during evening hours. The "prime time" should be reserved for tasks that require greatest creativity. "Down periods" can be reserved for less mentally demanding tasks such as running a routine experiment or transcribing notes. Once an effective schedule has been found, it should be maintained.

Unusual schedules should be considered carefully. Some students say they work best at night. This type of student may occasionally work throughout the night but is often missing from the department during the daytime hours. Unusual efforts such as these may be tolerated for extraordinary students, but for others, daytime hours are preferable, particularly if the advisor and the other members of the research group are active during the day.

It is useful to organize work-space areas and to learn how to properly order supplies and chemicals. Most universities have complicated rules for purchasing. A copy of the rules can be posted in the work area for reference. It is also important to learn about purchase orders so that checks can be made on orders that are delayed or canceled by vendors. Copies of all purchase orders should be kept for reference.

The time spent organizing research areas and learning rules may seem wasted, but this time will save many hours over a period of years. It is also important to determine what kind of help is available for scholarly and research work. If you are in a laboratory-based science, you will want to locate technical service shops that can be used for repair and construction of equipment. An advisor should be consulted about budgetary constraints that may limit the use of these services.

Many professors hire work-study students to perform routine clerical and laboratory tasks. Work-study students are typically undergraduates who are paid a nominal hourly wage for 10 to 20 hours per week. The federal government may furnish a large portion of the wages, with the balance provided through grants or departmental funds. Such funds may be available to the graduate researcher to hire a work-study student to do routine laboratory or literature work. This can save considerable time.

All researchers have to engage in routine tasks, but the time spent on these tasks can be used more effectively by simultaneously thinking about previous experiments and planning new experiments. For example, the neurobiologist setting up an electrophysiological experiment may mentally review the fundamentals of nerve function or methods that will be used to analyze the data to be collected during the impending experiment. A geologist collecting rock specimens in the field might give thought to crystal habits of commonly occurring minerals. The investigator on an archaeological dig might mentally survey the historical antecedents of the excavation site. This habit has been used by many professionals and is possibly a source of allusions to the "absentminded scholar." For example, Nathaniel Hawthorne developed ideas for four of his novels, including *The Scarlet Letter*, while performing routine duties in the Customs House in Salem, Massachusetts.[1] For a few years (1902–9) during Einstein's most creative period (1905–16), he worked eight hours a day at the Patent Office in Berne, Switzerland,[2] an intriguing fictionalized account of which was published in 1993.[3]

The effective use of work periods should relieve guilt about leisure time. In fact, time for personal interests and for relaxation can further professional interests, as suggested earlier. Nalimov noted that moments during the most trivial activities can provide useful insights from the subconscious or sudden spiked entries in the continuous consciousness.[4]

An informal survey of 14 prominent researchers and scholars at Washington State University suggested that idea-producing situations include showering, relaxing, golfing, swimming, and reading, among others.[5] Microbiologist William Rayburn gets ideas while showering, "the hotter the better." As the water splashes and steam rises, "I am writing letters in my mind, thinking about the data that I have just collected, maybe the day before or just last week, and then focusing on what I am going to do." The physicist George Duval believed in a theory he attributed to the nineteenth-century French mathematician Jacque Hadamard. Duval suggested that "you work very, very hard on the problem until you have all aspects in mind. Then you set it aside and lie on the beach, play a game of golf, or go skin diving. If things are going right, the solution to your problem will come to you." Biochemist Ralph Yount recommends general reading: "You have to read things totally irrelevant to your area, looking for tools or new ideas to apply to the problems that you have in hand." Thus, the times spent in sport and leisure can be viewed as opportunities for creative thought. Accordingly, pen and notepad should always be nearby to capture "brilliant" thoughts.

Execution

With goals set and routines organized, timely execution should be sought. The first step in executing tasks effectively is to identify time wasters. MacKenzie[6] listed the most common ones as follows:

1. Telephone interruptions
2. Ineffective use of the telephone
3. Visitors dropping in without notice
4. Crisis situations
5. Lack of deadlines
6. Not sticking to high-priority work
7. Indecision and procrastination
8. Over-involvement with detail and routine
9. Attempting too much
10. Underestimating the time needed to perform tasks
11. Poor communication
12. Inability to say "no"
13. Boredom, fatigue, and ill health

These time wasters can have a significant impact over a year, and ways should be found to minimize their influence. For example, voice-mail systems provide a method for minimizing telephone interruptions. Other potentially significant interruptions include visitors dropping by unannounced, although these encounters can sometimes lead to beneficial exchanges of ideas. Pelz and Andrews noted that generous interactions between scientists improve their effectiveness.[7] However, idle contacts or chitchat sessions are major time wasters. Friends who drop by every other morning to report on their latest feats in racquetball are performing a disservice. In discouraging intrusions of this type, body language is a useful aid. The intruder who is met at the door or greeted by your standing up is less likely to sit, relax, and proceed to waste 30 minutes of precious time. Similarly, overdrawn dialog is quickly brought to completion by standing up and walking with the person out of the room. Other assertiveness measures such as honestly noting a need to get back to work can be used with slower characters.

Deadlines improve performance. They provide some stress, or dither, that enhances creativity. Weaver adopted an unusual meaning for the word "dither."[8] He recounted how British engineers during World War II built a constant state of minor but rapid vibration into antiaircraft weaponry. It was thought that, if the guns were constantly in slight motion, this would free them from static friction and make them more responsive. For researchers and scholars, "dither" is a frequent state of mental excitement, which is perpetuated by deadlines and friendly jostling of ideas by colleagues. The mental excitement is largely self-controlled but is accentuated by deadlines set by external agencies (e.g., deadlines for submission of grant proposals).

Speed-reading is often suggested as a means of saving time. The scientist, however, must read carefully and slowly to weigh hypotheses and evaluate results and conclusions. While reading, consider the following questions: Was the experimental work well planned? Were the experiments carried out well? Are the conclusions supported by the data? What additional experimentation might be done to fully support the hypothesis? In coping with the tremendous increases in literature, priority consciousness in choosing reading material is more important than concern with reading faster.

Poor communications can result in serious time losses. Following are activities that can improve communications:

- Arrange regularly scheduled meetings with an advisor
- Organize appointments

- Take notes and use verbal feedback (e.g., "If I understand you correctly, you're saying that . . .") during research meetings

The remaining hindrances to effective time management are boredom, fatigue, and illness. Boredom is reduced by diversity. Blending experimentation with writing and studying is helpful. This type of diversity has been shown to benefit the productivity and creativity of scientists.[7] All work can be broken up by occasional personal rewards.

In summary, fulfilling plans for graduate and professional careers will require careful organization and execution. These are accomplished by using To Do Lists, establishing routines, arranging leisure activities, and minimizing time wasters. Efforts to improve time management will be of great help in completing experimental work, the principles of which are covered in the next chapter.

References

[1] A. Lakein, *How to Get Control of Your Time and Your Life* (New York: Signet, 1974).

[2] A. Pais, *"Subtle is the Lord . . .": The Science and Life of Albert Einstein* (London: Oxford University Press, 1982).

[3] A. Lightman, *Einstein's Dreams* (New York: Warner Books, 1993).

[4] V. V. Nalimov, *Realms of the Unconscious: The Enchanted Frontier* (Philadelphia: ISI Press, 1982).

[5] W. Stimson, Getting ideas, *Universe* 1 (1) (1988), pp. 10–11.

[6] R. A. MacKenzie, *The Time Trap* (New York: Amacon, 1990).

[7] D. C. Pelz and F. M. Andrews, *Scientists in Organizations. Productive Climates for Research and Development*, rev. ed. (Ann Arbor, MI: Institute for Social Research, University of Michigan, 1976).

[8] W. Weaver, Dither, *Science* 130 (1959), p. 301.

5 | PRINCIPLES OF SCIENTIFIC RESEARCH

Ever since the dawn of civilization, people have not been content to see events as unconnected and inexplicable. They have craved an understanding of the underlying order in the world. . . . Humanity's deepest desire for knowledge is justification enough for our continuing quest.

—Stephen Hawking

Scientific research has provided knowledge and understanding that can free humankind from the ignorance that once promoted fear, mysticism, superstition, and illness. Developments in science and scientific methods, however, did not come easily. Many of our ancestors had to face persecution, even death, from religious and political groups because they dared to advance the notion that knowledge and understanding could be gained through systematic study and practice.

Today, the benefits of scientific research are widely understood. We appreciate the advances in the biological and physical sciences that allow the control of environment, the probing of the universe, and communications around the globe. We also appreciate the advances in biochemistry and molecular biology that have led to curative drugs, to genetic counseling, and to an unparalleled understanding of structure-function relationships in living organisms. We look intriguingly to the development of life itself and, in concert with social-behavioral scientists, the unraveling of the relationship between mind and brain. Despite the potential moral issues raised by the latter advances, the history of science provides us faith that knowledge and understanding can be advanced for the benefit of humanity.

The methods for conducting scientific research that have been developed over the past centuries include the following:

- observation
- hypothesis

- experimentation
- interpretation

It is important to understand the nature of these methods and how each method should be used to conduct research.

Observations

There are two important roles for observations in scientific research. Initially, observations help define problems. Later, observations become critical elements in experimentation.

Medawar aptly noted, "Observation is not a passive imbibition of sensory information, a mere transcription of the evidences of the senses, . . . Observation is a critical and purposive process."[1] A conscious effort has to be made to observe and to develop a keen "eye" for things and events. This ability, new to many a beginning researcher, comes from raising one's consciousness and developing a questioning attitude. It is fostered by thoughtful reading and a desire to comprehend and integrate knowledge. The Nobel Laureate Linus Pauling noted, "Over the years I've built a picture of the world in my mind. And whenever I read about a new discovery or theory, I ask myself: 'Does this fit into my ideas about the universe?'"[2]

Like Pauling, the researcher constantly looks for answers to underlying questions. Molecular biologists, for example, automatically wonder about mechanisms of genetic expression, and they look for data that may provide clues. Biostatisticians will question how variables were treated in studies linking the incidence of heart disease to cigarette smoking. Marine biologists will question the accuracy of physical measurements in studies of the effects of acid rain on marine organisms. The thoughtful approach to observations, as exemplified, does not come easily because it is not stressed in undergraduate programs.

Undergraduates are accustomed to performing experiments exactly as described in laboratory manuals. Some students also get into the habit of studying just enough to score well on exams. Graduate education requires more thoughtful approaches and more dedication. It will take time to develop the background and perspective necessary to differentiate the old from the new, the profound from the mundane. The guidance of faculty and senior colleagues through core courses and individual research problem courses will help, but independent study and a determination to succeed will be necessary to become a scholar and researcher.

Early in one's graduate career, there may be frustration because of an apparent lack of problems to solve. This feeling is common to novice researchers. It has been experienced by some of the best scientists. Herbert C. Brown, 1979 Nobel Laureate in chemistry, reflected on his early perspective: "In 1936 when I received my B.S. degree, I felt that organic chemistry was a relatively mature science, with essentially all of the important reactions and structures known. There appeared to be little new to be done except the working out of reaction mechanisms and the improvement of reaction yields. I now recognize that I was wrong. I have seen major reactions discovered. . . . Many new structures are known."[3] Brown's progress as a researcher undoubtedly included attempts to improve observations. After making meaningful observations and becoming more introspective about science, researchers are ready to tackle the next step in the research process—developing hypotheses.

Hypotheses

A hypothesis is an imaginative preconception of a factual relationship. It comes from meaningful observations and takes the form of statements such as "Phenomenon A is related to phenomenon B through variable C." This concept of hypotheses was not always in force. The ancient Greeks, for example, believed that hypotheses were perfect and experimentation must confirm them. During the Dark Ages, a hypothesis was thought to be perfect and sufficient for gaining knowledge so long as it was blessed by theology and authority. Experimentation was unnecessary. It was not until the nineteenth century that great scientists like Louis Pasteur recommended that hypotheses be regarded as invaluable guides to action that could be discredited only by positive experimental evidence.

Hypotheses have also been referred to as theoretical generalizations, which should be contrasted with empirical generalizations that are summary statements of fact. An example of an empirical generalization might be, "Chameleons assume the color of their environments." This is different from a hypothesis on chameleon behavior, as indicated below. The importance of the hypothesis in determining truth should be emphasized. Without hypotheses, the scientific process can become a mere collection of data. Rosalyn Yalow, Nobel Laureate in medicine, noted, "Science is not simply a collection of facts; it is a discipline of thinking about rational solutions to problems after establishing the basic facts derived from observations. It is hypothesizing from what is known to what might be, and then attempting to test the hypothesis."[4]

It is important to differentiate between the research hypothesis and the null hypothesis, which maintains that the effect and cause are unrelated except by chance. An original hypothesis could be that drug A is more active biologically than drug B. The null hypothesis states that there is no difference in the biological activities of the two drugs and any difference found is due to random error (chance). The null hypothesis is useful in statistics because it is more easily tested than the original hypothesis.

How are research hypotheses developed? One of the best ways is to pursue ideas through literature work and to design relevant pilot experiments. Careful literature research is needed to avoid "reinventing the wheel." Also, extensive reading will lead to a refinement of ideas and to the development of new concepts. Indeed, a wide range of literature—including the popular press—can be useful. In the press, however, the "what happened?" *may* be accurate while the "why" and "how" *may* be fantastic. Hypothetical statements should be sought when reading, especially in the introductory sections of articles. In particular, authors of review articles and papers from scientific meetings may speculate on the feasibility of a hypothesis where literature evidence from diverse sources points to a congruence of ideas. Antecedents to model hypotheses are described below.

The development of hypotheses is aided by three principles:[5]

- Method of agreement
- Method of difference
- Concomitant variation

The *method of agreement* states that if an event with circumstances having one factor in common is repeated, the factor may be the cause of the event. Thus, it would seem obvious to hypothesize that a certain virus causes respiratory infections in mice if separate batches of the animals showed typical respiratory symptoms after repeated exposure to the suspected agent. On the other hand, the researcher can be misled by this seemingly obvious cause-and-effect relationship. What if the symptoms are caused by some irritant simultaneously administered with the virus? What if the viral suspensions are contaminated with infectious bacteria? These questions can be addressed only through controlled experimentation.

The *method of difference* states that if an event is repeated with one factor but not another, the first factor is the causative agent. Looking at the earlier infectious disease problem, experiments might be conducted with two fluids: one specially treated to remove viruses and the other untreated. A lack of respiratory symptoms in animals exposed to the treated fluid plus the regular appearance of symptoms in animals exposed to the untreated fluid would implicate the virus as a causative agent.

The third principle, *concomitant variation*, states that if an increase in the intensity of a factor is followed by a parallel variation in effect, then the factor is the cause of the event. Again, returning to the mouse experiments, different groups of animals could be subjected to increasing levels of viruses. A graded increase in the incidence and severity of respiratory symptoms would suggest a cause-and-effect relationship between the virus and respiratory infections.

It should be pointed out that the above noted experiments do not categorically eliminate coincident effects of bacteria or irritants; however, Occam's razor (preferring the simplest explanation that agrees with all the evidence) suggests that the virus is the cause of observed symptoms in mice. Nevertheless, we are still at the stage of hypothesis development. Experimentation is the obligatory next step.

Once a hypothesis is developed, its feasibility may be determined through pilot experimentation. Pilot work is important to conserve resources, and positive results from this effort will help motivate the extensive experimentation that must follow. I recall a turning point in one student's graduate work where a set of pilot experiments revealed the likelihood that the underlying hypothesis of the doctoral dissertation was correct. This Ph.D. research concerned the chemical transformations of the aromatic hydrocarbon *trans*-stilbene in mammals. Earlier literature had suggested that the estrogenic effect of this chemical in rabbits was caused by biotransformation products, yet relevant types of products had not been detected. The underlying hypothesis was that the products were in fact formed in rabbits and perhaps other animals but were not previously detected because of inadequate analytical methods. The pilot work required development of a simple analytical test for the expected products and an analysis of urine from a small group of rabbits administered *trans*-stilbene. Results of these preliminary experiments were positive. It took more than a year of subsequent experimentation to prove the hypothesis through careful experiments in more rabbits and two other species of animals. The feeling of accomplishment and hope from the pilot work, however, was of inestimable value to the student in developing the necessary perseverance to complete the doctoral work.

A caveat concerning pilot experimentation is that one can become carried away with it. Pilot experiments are not too rigorously executed, and this may serve as a temptation to continue experimentation carelessly. Some students never seem to get beyond a string of less rigorously performed "preliminary experiments." Pilot experimentation has its place. It is no substitute, however, for definitive experimentation.

The literature work and pilot experimentation may be done. The hypothesis must then emerge. Following are examples of hypotheses that could have been developed by three different graduate students.

- A zoology graduate researcher might hypothesize:

"The American chameleon assumes the color of its environment because of unique structural changes in its skin pigments."

Statements may have been found in the literature suggesting that chameleon skin-pigment molecules are capable of undergoing structural changes. Other literature citations could have pointed to the likelihood of varying light absorption characteristics of chemical compounds resembling chameleon pigments. Pilot experiments might have indicated that changes in solution composition alter the visible light absorption characteristics of model pigments.

- A civil engineering graduate student might hypothesize:

"Bridges made of vanadium steel are sturdier than those constructed of carbon steel."

Reports in the metallurgical literature may have contained stress-strain curves for vanadium steel suggesting that the component atoms align and relax upon stress in a way that might prevent fatigue and cracking. Pilot experiments with the two types of steel might have suggested improved strength characteristics for vanadium steel bars.

- A psychology graduate student might hypothesize:

"Sensory impairment in human subjects is associated with increased social isolation and is manifested by clinical depression."

Articles in professional magazines for clinical psychologists might have described experiences of practitioners providing services to hearing- and sight-impaired clients. A pilot survey of hearing- or sight-impaired widows and of widows with normal hearing and sight might have suggested a greater incidence of depression in the former subjects.

Good hypotheses should be testable in a practical and a theoretical sense. The hypothesis testing should not require establishment of a new laboratory or the investment of millions of dollars. Also, equipment (e.g., spectrometers, computers) and research tools (e.g., statistical methods, survey instruments) must be available or readily developed for collecting and analyzing data that will be generated during experimentation.

The researcher should consider other practical limitations. Desirable equipment for testing a hypothesis may not be available. However, equipment might be borrowed or leased, or alternative methods might be adopted for achieving the same results. For example, a biologist may be aware of a radioactive tracer technique for studying a physiological process, but the equipment necessary to use the method may not be available in an advisor's laboratory. A less convenient or more time-consuming approach might be adopted that provides equally valid data. In summary, the hypothesis is a preconception of outcomes, it is testable, and it is the primary basis for experimentation.

Experimentation

The researcher makes things happen through experimentation! This would have been a strange idea to early scientists, who believed that discoveries were made by observing nature and waiting for events to occur in a certain juxtaposition so that truth would be revealed. In the early 1600s, Sir Francis Bacon suggested that people must make their opportunities as often as find them.[1] Bacon's contemporary, Galileo Galilei, was among the first proponents of the critical experiment—one that discriminates between narrow possibilities.[1] After Pasteur's work in the late 1800s, experiments became accepted as a test or trial of a hypothesis.

Besides hypotheses, modern experimentation is marked by quantitative measurement. As noted by Lord Kelvin more than a century ago: "When you can measure what you are speaking about and express it in numbers, you know something about it. And when you cannot measure it, when you cannot express it in numbers, your knowledge is of a meager and unsatisfactory kind. It may be the beginning of knowledge, but you have scarcely in your thought advanced to the stage of a science."[6] Many years before Kelvin, Pythagoras stated more succinctly, "Mathematics is the way to understand the universe. . . . Number is the measure of all things."[7]

In addition to quantitative measurements, experiments must be subject to controls. The results of experiments are never the sum total of all that is observed. Rather, a simple one-factor experiment will involve comparing the measurement of a dependent variable in the test situation to the control condition where the effect of this variable is small or nil. The result is the difference between the two conditions—experiment minus control. More complicated (multiple-factor) experiments can be performed to measure effects of more than one dependent variable, but suitable controls must be instituted for each.

Good experimentation is marked by methodical planning and execution. The planning must include considerations such as: numbers of experimental subjects and controls, use of standards, sampling procedures and sample labeling, equipment calibration, treatment conditions at strategically chosen values for experimental variables, and methods of analysis, including statistical tests.[8] The civil engineering student mentioned earlier, for example, would consider several factors in designing experiments to test his or her hypothesis that bridges made of vanadium steel are sturdier than those constructed of carbon steel. Initially, samples of the two types of steel would be obtained and tests performed to confirm their composition. This would require some type of chemical analysis. The steels would then be used to construct model bridges, which would be subjected to stress-strain measurements. All equipment would be calibrated to determine the accuracy (how close actual values are to theoretical values) and precision (the variability in repeated measurements with the same equipment and under the same conditions) of the measurement steps. The conditions of the stress-strain determinations, such as temperature, period of stress, degree of stress, and points of stress, would be defined. The measurements obtained would be treated statistically to determine possible significant differences between the bridge types.

The design of experiments is a science unto itself. Good execution, on the other hand, requires practice much like that of a concert pianist. The practice can be thought of as the "art of experimentation." Novice researchers often harbor the fantasy that a few offhand observations and experiments will bring success. As noted earlier, experimentation provides little instant gratification. It takes commitment and hard work to achieve results.

One way to improve execution in experimentation is to attempt model experiments or to repeat the work of a predecessor. Experienced research advisors know this and will often assign some of the completed work of a former graduate student. This assignment serves two purposes: it helps to develop technique and build confidence, and it provides an additional opportunity to test the results of the previous investigation. As one chemistry professor noted, "I am reluctant to publish results until experiments have been performed successfully by more than one graduate student."

Alternatively, a newly proposed experiment may be tried initially with a simpler system—one in which the prediction of success is high. This is common practice, for example, with organic chemists who plan the synthesis of a complex natural product. After inspecting the target molecule, the chemist proposes ways of constructing it in stages from less and less complex starting materials. The resulting total synthesis scheme may require more than 10 steps, many of which may not occur readily and may require the use of rare starting materials. In these instances, a model reaction with less complex compounds may be performed to determine the potential usefulness of a proposed chemical reaction step. If the reaction is successful, further reactions with the same model compounds may be performed to improve product yields. When conditions have been optimized, the parallel reaction is run with the rare starting materials.

A successful approach to complex experimental problems is to break them up into several smaller experiments and to complete the work in parts. The "parts" are then ordered through subhypotheses and tackled so the easiest experiments are performed first. In the *trans*-stilbene project, for example, the work beyond pilot experiments was subdivided. After developing methods for detecting metabolites in urine, additional analytical procedures were devised to determine the concentrations of metabolites in urine. Procedures were also developed to confirm the structural formulae of metabolites. Evidence for the proposed metabolites in rabbits encouraged experiments in two other species of mammals: mice and guinea pigs.

Quantitative analysis of the *trans*-stilbene metabolites in rabbits, mice, and guinea pigs indicated problems with mass balance determinations. That is, the total amounts of metabolites formed did not correspond to the amounts of *trans*-stilbene administered. This prompted hypotheses about alternative pathways of biotransformation and excretion that were subsequently studied by other students. Thus, results of experiments led to new hypotheses, which in turn led to new experiments. One dissertation project led to others. This is the nature of scientific research.

Like all research, the *trans*-stilbene work was often difficult and tedious. It was important, therefore, for the student to order the experiments so that the easiest steps were accomplished first. Sometimes one hears a statement like this: "If I can accomplish the most difficult experiment first, then all the rest will be easy." This is most often a nonsensical idea that can lead to unnecessary failure and despair. Usually it is more sensible to progress from easier to harder experiments, although pilot and model experiments of more difficult stages of the research are frequently helpful, as noted earlier.

In some areas of research (e.g., evolutionary botany, environmental science), subjects and conditions of experimentation are not readily controllable as they are in laboratory-based research. For such studies, computer modeling and other multivariant approaches may be necessary to tease out hypothesized interrelationships.

Developing protocols for initial experiments can be helpful to beginning researchers. These strict sets of directions for experiments list details on materials and methods. The student psychologist interested in hearing- and sight-impaired subjects, for example, might prepare a protocol for a major experiment by addressing the following questions:

1. How many subjects will be needed in the experimental and control groups?
2. How will subjects be recruited and how will informed consent be obtained?
3. What instrument(s) (questionnaire) is suitable for the study?
4. What are the psychometric characteristics (e.g., reliability, stability, and validity) of the instrument(s)?
5. Under what conditions will the questionnaire be administered?
6. How will subject confidentiality be protected during and after the study?
7. How will the questionnaire responses be scored and the results analyzed?
8. What level of significance is necessary to accept the hypothesis or reject the null hypothesis?

The complete protocol would be reviewed with the student's advisor prior to implementation. Since the protocol involves human subjects, the study would also require review by the human subjects review committee of the university (see Chapter 11).

If the psychology researcher found that clinical depression was statistically more common or more severe in sensory-impaired subjects, the following questions for new hypotheses might arise:

1. Is the difference age-dependent?
2. Are there differences in types and severity of depression between sensory-impaired men and women?

3. What effects can spouses or significant others have on the course of treatment for depression?
4. Is the treatment of depression as effective in sensory-impaired patients as it is in subjects with normal hearing and vision?
5. Are differential results likely when comparing psychotherapy with pharmacotherapy?

Thus, research leads to research. Acceptance of one hypothesis leads to other hypotheses and, perhaps, the development of theories. The process of "theory-building," however, must be a dynamic one. As noted by the great theoretical physicist Stephen Hawking, "Each time new experiments are observed to agree with the predictions the theory survives, and our confidence in it is increased; but if ever a new observation is found to disagree, we have to abandon or modify the theory."[9]

The best stimulus for achieving research goals is initial success. Indeed, until something of worth is accomplished, there may be frequent crises of incentive. Dedication is particularly necessary at first to achieve some measure of success later. Once new researchers have one or two satisfying accomplishments behind them, future experimental efforts (even with unavoidable failures) can be faced more optimistically. After new researchers have reached a certain stage of accomplishment, then and only then are they able to begin each day with the thought, "Even if everything goes wrong today, I have something to fall back on." This feeling of confidence enables researchers to apply themselves effectively, and, inevitably, other successful experiments follow. This feeling also inspires greater and greater confidence.

A fantasy that plagues new researchers is success by chance. That is, some unexplained event will occur that is highly significant. Chance or serendipity (allegedly derived from Horace Walpole's land of "Serendip" where fortunate accidents were the norm) does have a role to play in scientific discoveries, as indicated previously. However, it only works for the keen and experienced researcher.

Interesting examples of serendipity include the discovery of a moon of the planet Pluto, and the artificial sweetener aspartame, or Nutrasweet,® now commonly used in diet soft drinks.[10]

The astronomical discovery was made by James Christy at the U.S. Naval Observatory in 1978 and occurred during a telescopic study of Pluto's orbital characteristics. The observations were photographed, and in one photo the planet's image appeared elongated, possibly suggesting some fault with the measurement system. Further investigation, however, indicated that the elongation was caused not by an artifact but by a previously unknown moon (later named Charon) of the most distant planet in our solar system.

Aspartame, a simple dipeptide derivative (L-aspartyl-L-pheny-lalanine methyl ester) was synthesized originally at the G. D. Searle Company as part of a program designed to discover new anti-ulcer drugs. While handling this compound, a chemist noticed its sweet taste, which would not have been predicted based on its chemical structure.

To allow for serendipity and to properly engage in experimentation, one has to be open-minded. Also, one must not become so wedded to a hypothesis as to be blinded to the truth. Ira Remson, the first chairperson of the department of chemistry at Johns Hopkins University, noted: "Great harm has been done chemistry, and probably every other branch of knowledge, by unwarranted speculation, and everyone who has looked into the matter knows how extremely difficult it is to emancipate one's self from the influence of a plausible hypothesis even when it can be shown that it is not in accordance with the facts."[11] Experimentation must be carried out with the understanding that results will be accepted and interpreted according to how they happen.

Interpretation

Interpretation is developing meaning from the data that results when we test a hypothesis through experimentation. During the initial interpretative process it must be determined whether the data are consistent with the underlying hypothesis. Approaches include statistics, tabulating, plotting and visualizing data, library or other literature work, introspection, and discussions with an advisor and other faculty or colleagues.

Statistical analyses help in making objective judgments about differences in data sets and degrees of significance of differences. Statistics courses are very important additions to most graduate students' programs. Information on statistics texts is available through the *Computer Vision Handbook* maintained by Fleck and Stevenson at the University of Iowa's Computer Vision Laboratory.[12] Internet statistical resources have been nicely cataloged by Varnum and Weise at the University of Michigan School of Information and Library Studies.[13]

Tabulating and plotting data are also useful ways of seeing relationships in data. Indeed, most advisors will recommend these treatments for written reports and as aids in formal research conferences.

Interpretation is made easier by literature work and reflective thinking. One cannot hold to a timetable at this stage. When insight won't come, it is helpful to "forget" the problem for a while. A period of incubation may subsequently be followed by illumination, sometimes referred to as "aha! insight."[14] Such insight may come at unusual times such as dozing or waking, during periods of personal hygiene or evacuation, or when traveling. The psychologist Julian Jaynes referred to these times as the three B's—the bed, the bath, and the bus.[15]

The social scientist Walt Rostow related the unusual timing of his inspiration for his 1983 economics book: "At 3:00 a.m. on the morning of December 15, 1982, when sleep was light, I got up and outlined this book just about in the form that it now appears."[16] Similarly, a Manager of Innovation and Technology Development at the Battelle Pacific Northwest National Laboratory (formerly the Battelle Pacific Northwest Laboratories) noted that "one must pay attention to the subconscious. If I don't write down an idea that comes to me, I have great difficulty reconstructing it. So I have a pad of paper beside my bed, and I will write down ideas that come to me in the middle of the night."[17]

Examples abound for inspiration during moments of personal hygiene or traveling. Einstein was frequently inspired while shaving. The eminent chemist Karl Folkers described the traveling incident during which he first became convinced of a structural formula for penicillin: "On the train from Chicago to Madison, I sat there, looking out the window, . . . As I reviewed the evidence in my mind about the beta-lactam formulas, they sounded pretty good. . . . It was on that trip that for the first time in my participation in the penicillin program, that I really took the beta-lactam seriously."[18] The physicist Tom Dickinson noted, "For me, some targeted idea-generators come from reading a journal article or sitting in a talk at a professional meeting or a departmental colloquium. Untargeted activity, such as letting one's mind wander during a walk or run, is sometimes more intense and fruitful."[19]

These tales mirror the experiences of many others. Researchers often develop some of their best ideas while traveling to and from meetings. Oddly enough, just as the astronauts had to leave the earth to see its grandeur for the "first time," the solutions to local problems are frequently found by "leaving" them. New researchers should be aware of the potential influence of the three B's on insight. This will help significantly.

Once an interpretation for data is developed, it must be subjected to the scrutiny of others. Here, other graduate students and certainly an advisor are important. Ultimately, research results and interpretations will be presented at research group meetings and regional and national conferences, and will be prepared for publication in peer-reviewed journals. This pattern of review and critique serves as a basis for the self-correcting process that is essential in science.

The successful researcher lives a life of observations, hypotheses, experimentation, and interpretation. This requires integrity and an understanding of ethical behavior, which are discussed in the next chapter.

References

[1] P. B. Medawar, *Advice to a Young Scientist* (New York: Harper and Row, 1979).

[2] J. Kitfield, Laureates—Linus Pauling, *Northwest Orient* 17 (1) (1986), pp. 37–39.

[3] H. C. Brown, Adventures in research, *Chemical and Engineering News* 59 (14) (1981), pp. 24–29.

[4] Rosalyn S. Yalow, Melange: Commencement 1988, *The Chronicle of Higher Education* 34 (39) (1988), p. B-3.

[5] E. B. Wilson, Jr., *An Introduction to Scientific Research* (New York: McGraw-Hill, 1952).

[6] W. Thomson (Lord Kelvin), *Popular Lectures and Addresses by Sir William Thomson, 1891–1894* (New York: Macmillan, 1894).

[7] R. W. Hamming, The unreasonable effectiveness of mathematics, *American Mathematics Monthly* 87 (2) (1980), pp. 81–90.

[8] Commission on Physical Sciences, Mathematics, and Resources, National Academy of Sciences, *Improving the Treatment of Scientific and Engineering Data Through Education* (Washington, D.C.: National Academy Press, 1986).

[9] S. W. Hawking, *A Brief History of Time* (New York: Bantam Books, 1988).

[10] R. M. Roberts, *Serendipity—Accidental Discoveries in Science* (New York: Wiley, 1989).

[11] A. H. Corwin, in *Proceedings of the Robert A. Welch Conference on Chemical Research. XX. American Chemistry Bicentennial*, W. O. Milligan, ed. (Houston, TX: Robert A. Welch Foundation, 1977), pp. 45–69.

[12] M. Fleck and D. Stevenson, *The Computer Vision* (Iowa City: University of Iowa, Computer Vision Laboratory, Computer Science Department, 1996); http://www.cs.uiowa.edu/~mfleck/vision-html/handbook/statistics.html

[13] K. Varnum and J. Weise, *A Guide to Statistical Computing Resources on the Internet* (Ann Arbor, MI: University of Michigan School of Information and Library Studies, 1994); http://asa.ugl.lib.umich.edu/chdocs/statistics/stat_guide_home.html

[14] M. Gardner, *Aha! Insight* (New York: Scientific American, 1978).

[15] J. Jaynes, *The Origin of Consciousness in the Breakdown of the Bicameral Mind* (Boston: Houghton Mifflin, 1976).

[16] W. W. Rostow, *The Barbaric Counterrevolution: Cause and Cure* (Austin, TX: University of Texas Press, 1983).

[17] E. A. Eschbach, Fostering creativity, *PNL Profile* (Fall 1986), pp. 9–10; Battelle Pacific Northwest Laboratories, *Document BN-FA 530, Updated 3-88*, Creativity, discovery, invention and the put-down.

[18] J. C. Sheehan, *The Enchanted Ring: The Untold Story of Penicillin* (Cambridge, MA: MIT Press, 1982).

[19] T. Dickinson, The importance of junk piles, *Universe* 5 (1) (1992), p. 11.

6 | ETHICS AND THE SCIENTIST

The only ethical principle which has made science possible is that truth shall be told all the time. . . . And of course a false statement of fact, made deliberately, is the most serious crime a scientist can commit.

—C. P. Snow

Three principles are cast in the ethos and methods of modern science: the pursuit of truth, freedom to pursue truth, and reverence for all life forms and the environment. These principles are consistent with scientists' values and are upheld by integrity, a respect for liberty, and a commitment to preservation.

Science and its ethical underpinnings are threatened by deception, delusion, and dishonesty. These elements of the dark side of science are manifest as research misconduct. Science's dark side must be understood and its manifestations prevented. Graduate researchers should also understand the ethical expectations of university communities regarding the development and protection of intellectual property.

The Ethos and Methods of Science

Good science requires integrity, freedom of inquiry, and reverence for life and the environment. These principles have not always been upheld by scientists. Critics point to instances of misconduct, obsequiousness to devious military and political forces, and disregard for human and animal life and the environment as failures of the scientific community. Scientists are now aware that past failures cannot be repeated. We have to police ourselves or else governmental bodies will assume the task exclusively. Fortunately, the scientific method and scientists' values assist the scientific community in living up to its principles.

The scientific method—consisting of observations, hypotheses, experimentation, and interpretation—is dependent upon integrity. Integrity is essential for individual research efforts—integrity and trust undergird the universality of scientific results. Integrity, upheld by most scientists, provides courage to face failures and to accept evidence that runs counter to hypotheses and existing theories. These seemingly obvious truths about integrity are the basis for the astonishment experienced by most scientists when they learn of dishonesty in science. Most researchers cannot imagine how anyone could conduct research without honest approaches to its methods. Such approaches include attempts to minimize error and to correct errors once they are detected.

Besides the importance of integrity, part of the attraction of science is the joy of discovery and the feelings of accomplishment derived from finding evidence to support hypotheses and theories. Bias, cheating, and dishonesty defeat these purposes and are in direct opposition to the values held by most scientists.

Scientists' Values

The sociologist Milton Rokeach and his colleagues spent many years studying human values, which they defined as beliefs that serve as preferences for action. Rokeach et al. developed a dual survey system to measure terminal values (i.e., held for long periods and until late in life) and instrumental values (i.e., leading to modes of behavior) of various groups of individuals.[1-3]

When university biological, physical, and social scientists (N = 152) were surveyed, the five top-rated terminal values found were (1) sense of accomplishment, (2) self-respect, (3) wisdom (defined as a mature understanding of life based on arts and sciences), (4) family security, and (5) freedom (4 and 5 were tied).[1] When average Americans (N = 1,409) were surveyed, the top five values found were (1) a world at peace, (2) family security, (3) freedom, (4) happiness, and (5) self-respect. For comparison purposes, average Americans rate "sense of accomplishment" as 10th and "wisdom" as 6th in a list of 18 terminal values. Interestingly, average Americans rate salvation as 8th while university biological, physical, and social scientists list it as 18th, or as the least important of the terminal values.

An analogous study of instrumental values of biological, physical, and social scientists revealed the following set: (1) honest,

(2) capable, (3) intellectual, (4) broadminded, and (5) responsible. In contrast, average Americans' top five instrumental values were (1) honest, (2) ambitious, (3) responsible, (4) forgiving, and (5) broadminded. And, for comparison purposes, average Americans rated "capable" as 9th and "intellectual" as 15th.

As noted by Rokeach, "College professors place considerably more value on intellectual competence and self-actualization than do adult Americans, whereas adult Americans generally care considerably more for God, home, country, and material things." Also, the values expressed by biological, physical, and social scientist faculty "seem [to be] . . . determined by selective factors that predispose one to an academic career or by socialization in graduate school rather than after recruitment to a faculty position."[1] Thus, value development is important in graduate school. For, as Rokeach et al. believed, one's values can not only be defined through self-confrontation and testing, but apparent contradictions can be the basis for changes in one's behavior or set of values.[1-3]

The value pattern of "intellectual competence and self-actualization" of university scientists helps to explain many of the characteristics, attitudes, and behaviors of scientists described in earlier chapters. This pattern, in conjunction with the value placed on "honesty," which is shared equally with adult Americans, undergirds the desirable characteristics of scientific research: integrity, a search for truth, and objectivity. Furthermore, responsible scientists know that these characteristics would not be possible without tough and sometimes critical review. The reviews begin in graduate school through critiques of presentations at research group meetings and research reports prepared for advisors. Critiques continue as thesis or dissertation chapters are written and reviewed by faculty committees, and when papers are presented at conferences or submitted for publication. This is the character of science and some of the bases for the so-called self-correcting nature of scientific research. This notion of "self-correction" is another reason why most scientists are surprised to learn of dishonesty by some unscrupulous researchers.

There are counterpoints to the above discussion of scientists' values and activities in research. Namely, a scientist's quest for "intellectual competence and self-actualization" can lead to arrogance and narcissism. Furthermore, overconfidence in the "self-correcting" nature of science can backfire, as evidenced by some of the extraordinary cases of research misconduct that have been noted throughout history. Researchers must understand that scientists, and even some seemingly good scientists, can pass into the dark side of science.

The Dark Side of Science

High standards, critical reviews, accomplishments, and deadlines are some of the stresses involved in scientific research. These stresses are essential for excellence in research, but they must be leavened by values such as integrity, self-respect, and objectivity, lest one be trapped by the doors leading to the dark side of science: deception, delusion, and dishonesty.[4]

Deception, especially self-deception, is the use of incomplete, misleading, or biased information. Researchers deceive themselves and society by altering irregularities in data to make the results look more accurate and precise and by dropping data or ignoring data that do not seem to fit a presupposed set of conclusions.[5] Other deceptive practices include making experiments appear more thorough than they actually were by implying precautions that were not taken or adhered to, or by implying more perfected methodology than was used, or through the purposeful use of inappropriate statistical tests.[6] The above types of deception may be caused by carelessness, inadequate intro-spection, laziness, or uncritical review of one's work.[7]

Deceptive scientists may also engage in shoddy publication prac-tices such as duplicative publication, unnecessary or excessive subdi-vision of papers into "least publishable units," and irresponsible authorship.[8] The last deception includes unjustified authorship (ac-knowledging as authors individuals who did not have a substantial part in the research represented by a paper) and incomplete author-ship (not acknowledging those who have contributed substantially to research leading to a paper). Regardless of causes, all deceptive prac-tices are unacceptable and can lead to delusions.

Delusion is belief in falsehood and an unwillingness to accept new and nonconfirmatory information. Scientists who practice de-ception may begin to believe their own deceit. The resulting delusion may arise from an unwillingness to accept failure due to closed-mindedness, arrogance, or a pernicious desire to succeed or achieve fame. Delusions are amplified when scientists become immune to criti-cism from colleagues and peers. Ultimately, delusions lead to outright dishonesty.

Dishonesty is the willful and malicious use of false or stolen in-formation. Dishonest scientists are those who plagiarize or otherwise misappropriate[9] others' work; fabricate data or other results; conduct research that violates laws pertaining to the use of animals, biohazards, or human subjects (see Chapter 11); or violate confidentiality in the handling of papers and grant proposals intended for review only. Dishonesty arises from a pathological personality, which is often manifested in manipulative aggressive behavior. The pathological personality "sees" all problems as someone else's fault or the fault of the institution, system, or other external agents. Similarly, the person who commits scientific misconduct often excuses himself or herself by saying something like, "I was under so much pressure from my supervisor's demands and the need to complete my project that I found these actions necessary." In actuality, these types of excuses elicit no sympathy. There are no acceptable reasons for dishonesty in science. Researchers must understand this.

Fortunately, the honesty of most researchers is impeccable, and deception, delusion, and dishonesty appear to be relatively rare in science. But new researchers must be careful to differentiate between honest mistakes, on the one hand, and passage through the doors of science's dark side, on the other.

Novice researchers may misunderstand experimental errors and variance, or how these factors are manifest in different kinds of studies. For example, analytical chemists may expect precision errors of $\pm 1\%$ when determining the sodium chloride content of an electrolyte solution. Clinical pharmacologists, in contrast, commonly observe $\pm 50\%$ variations in responses of patients to drugs. It is important to learn about experimental errors, variations, and proper data treatment for one's area of research. This background can be obtained through experimental methods courses, through the guidance of advisors, and the examples of role models. Such background is essential to success and to fulfilling the responsibility of all scientists to police their ranks and report observed misconduct in research.[10]

Misconduct in Research

Historians have uncovered examples of deception, delusion, and dishonesty, even among some of the greats of science, including Pascal (seventeenth century), Newton (eighteenth century), and Millikan (twentieth century), all three of whom allegedly misrepresented or dropped data; Lavoisier (eighteenth century), who allegedly stole ideas from Joseph Priestly; and Noguchi (twentieth century), who manufactured data on the isolation and cultivation of human pathogenic microorganisms.[5, 11–15] Since 1960, there have been many well-publicized cases of misconduct in science, including the alleged famous and the infamous: Mark Spector (graduate student cancer researcher who concocted a theory of cancer etiology), William Summerlin (associate professor immunologist who faked skin grafts in animals through inking), and John Darsee (assistant professor cardiology researcher who made up data for biomedical research papers).[14-16]

It would be comforting to say that all of these instances of deception, delusion, or outright dishonesty were brought to justice. Unfortunately, some cases (e.g., Noguchi) were only revealed after the scientists had completed seemingly successful careers and died. Other cases, however, were detected in a timely manner through the scrutiny of colleagues or the inability of peers to repeat results, and the revelations caused the disgrace and downfall of the guilty parties (e.g., Spector, Summerlin, and Darsee).

Given the recent attention to misconduct in science, it is probably safe to conclude that future cases of dishonesty will be investigated and prosecuted with vigor. In fact, due in part to federal guidelines published in 1989, most universities have spent considerable effort during the past several years developing policies and procedures to deal with misconduct in research.[17] In many institutions, misconduct is defined as:[18]

1. The falsification or fabrication of data; plagiarism and other deviations from accepted practice during the proposing, implementing, or reporting of research
2. The failure to comply with federal, state, or university requirements for (a) the protection of the public, human subjects, and researchers during research; and (b) ensuring the welfare of laboratory animals
3. The use of research funds, facilities, or staff for unauthorized or illegal activities
4. Conflicts of interest between researchers and sponsors of research in the conduct or reporting of research.

What is the incidence of misconduct in research as defined above? In 1988, Swazey et al. conducted a survey of research misconduct, which included most major U.S. universities.[19] Of the 259 institutions providing usable returns, 40% reported receiving one to five reports of faculty misconduct during the previous five years. Only six institutions received more than five reports during the five-year period. Of the total reported cases of faculty misconduct, only 20% were verified.

Regarding graduate student misconduct in research, 40% of the responding institutions had 1 to 5 cases of alleged misconduct during the previous five years, but 13 institutions had 6 to 15 cases of alleged misconduct. The rate of verified graduate student misconduct was about 30%. Thus, there were a few hundred cases of misconduct in research during the period 1983–88, at 259 universities, which collectively had hundreds of thousands of faculty and graduate students in the sciences. Results of this study suggested that the incidence of misconduct in research at these universities was much less than 1%.

Subsequent surveys in the early 1990s by Swazey et al.[20] and the American Association for the Advancement of Science (AAAS)[21] suggested that research misconduct may not be as rare among faculty and graduate students as indicated by earlier work. In the former study, 6–9% of faculty and students surveyed (1,440 doctoral students and 1,180 faculty at 99 departments in chemistry, civil engineering, microbiology, and sociology at U.S. research universities) signaled direct knowledge of faculty who had plagiarized work or falsified research results. More disturbingly, nearly one-third of the faculty surveyed had observed plagiarism by graduate students.

In the AAAS study, 27% of 469 respondent members indicated that they had detected or witnessed fabricated, falsified, or plagiarized research on an average of 2.5 times during the previous 10 years. Of this group, 37% chose to speak privately with the alleged offenders. However, 27% of the observants chose to do nothing!

These latter survey results are discomforting, but it is instructive to note that they deal primarily with allegations and not results of institutional investigations. Nevertheless, perusal of annual reports of federal agencies responsible for significant research funding (e.g., the National Institutes of Health[22]) indicates a greater incidence of research misconduct than would be expected for professionals who espouse the values of science enumerated above. As suggested by Broad, it is not the frequency of misconduct in research that is remarkable, but the fact that it occurs at all given the ethos and methods of science.[13]

The nature of misrepresentation of data has been noted earlier. However, it is important to elaborate further on plagiarism, since this brand of misconduct is most frequently observed among graduate students. Plagiarism has been defined as "taking credit for someone else's work and ideas, stealing others' results or methods, copying the writing of others without acknowledgment, or otherwise taking credit falsely."[7] Accordingly, it is important for researchers to cite others' work properly and to obtain permission for the use of published material. Sentences or phrases lifted verbatim from others' work must be presented as quotations with the source cited. Large sections of material such as paragraphs, tables, or figures can be used only after receiving permission from the copyright holder(s).

A copyright is a right of protection or monopoly for a piece of literature or art, and it exists whether or not an application has been filed with the Register of Copyrights. The specifications of copyrights vary with circumstances, but for newly created work, the term is usually the author's life plus 50 years. The permission to use copyrighted or other printed materials must be obtained in writing from the copyright owner by using a letter with format similar to the one indicated in Figure 6-1. Ethics also require that courtesy approval be sought from the author of material to be reproduced, even if the author has assigned the copyright to some other agent (e.g., a publishing firm). Permission for cartoons may require letters to publishing syndicates, addresses for which are found in *Literary Market Place*.[23]

Research misconduct related to compliance with federal, state, or university requirements for the protection of animals, human subjects, the public, and other researchers during research is avoided by following the recommendations provided in Chapter 11.

Misconduct in science through unauthorized or illegal use of research funds, facilities, or staff needs little elaboration. However, it should be noted that there are strict federal debarment policies that place advisors' federal grants and, indeed, an institution's entire federal funding program in jeopardy if research funds are used illegally. Thus, the stakes are high for infractions.

University policies on conflict of interest relate to (1) the nature and extent of consulting or other work permitted outside of the university; (2) involvement of personnel with firms that may sponsor research at the university, particularly if the research may lead to commercial products; and (3) publication, patenting, and licensing of intellectual property resulting from research. Of particular interest here are documentation, disclosure, ownership, and revenue-sharing (i.e., from licensing fees and royalties) policies and procedures, copies of which should be obtained from central research offices (e.g., Vice Provost or Vice President for Research) if any of these activities apply to you or to research projects that you may pursue.

In summary, misconduct in research involves breaches of integrity that are damaging to the researcher and the institution. Furthermore, research misconduct damages our relationships with society, whose support for research through federal and state taxes is essential to scientists' quest for new knowledge. It is therefore in our best interest to ensure that researchers' attention and behavior match the principles and values we purportedly espouse.

Figure 6-1. Letter format for obtaining permission to publish copyrighted and other printed materials.

Address of Copyright
Owner or Author of Printed Material

Dear Sir/Madam:

I request permission to use published material for which I understand you own the copyright.

The copyrighted material I wish to use is as follows:

_____

My use of this material is to have it published in the following journal (book, etc.):

_____

The publisher will be:_____

Proper acknowledgment of copyright owner and date will be given in the work.

If you approve of my request, please indicate your permission by signing on the line below and returning this letter to me in the enclosed self-addressed stamped envelope. I enclose a duplicate copy of this letter for your records.

Thank you for your cooperation in this matter.

Sincerely,

Date: _____

Permission granted:

_____

Signature of copyright owner or agent

Keeping the Code

It should be apparent that ethics is not a subject that can be covered in a few pages of a book. Ethics, values, and preferred modes of behavior must be constantly reinforced. In much of the recent literature on ethics and misconduct in research, authors have emphasized the notion that researchers' consciousness of ethics must be raised if we are to prevent the reoccurrence of the ethical lapses of the past. How might this be done?

Certainly, additional reading is helpful, and the major works cited in this chapter are recommended along with papers published in the journal *Science and Engineering Ethics*[24] and ethics case studies published on the Programs to Enhance Professional Development www site.[25] Graduate researchers should also consider taking courses in ethics and recommending to advisors and other faculty that presentations on ethics be given during research group meetings or departmental seminars. Finally, thought should be given to the human attributes that reinforce commitments to ethical values and behavior.

It was suggested earlier that the doors to the dark side of science are greased by arrogance, narcissism, carelessness, closed-mindedness, laziness, thoughtlessness, and a pernicious desire to succeed. Such failings are counteracted by humility, unselfishness, thoughtfulness, liberal-mindedness, industriousness, kindness, and compassion. These virtues should be nurtured in all new researchers through the example of advisors, other faculty, and colleagues—to enhance personal well-being, to assist professional development, and to bolster the esprit de corps of research groups. Scientists, like all professionals, should learn that life is not all goals, achievements, and recognition. As noted by Leo Buscaglia, "Life is getting there."[26] To summarize succinctly, science needs toughness and kindness—in balanced and measured proportion.

This concludes a sequence of chapters on the commitments, choices, methods, and ethos of graduate researchers. It is now useful to consider skills that improve one's effectiveness in research. One set of skills is library and literature work, which is covered in the next chapter.

References

[1] M. Rokeach, *The Nature of Human Values* (New York: Free Press, 1973).

[2] M. Rokeach, *Understanding Human Values—Individual and Societal* (New York: Free Press, 1979).

[3] S. J. Ball-Rokeach, M. Rokeach, and J. W. Grube, *The Great American Values Test* (New York: Free Press, 1984).

[4] L. A. Shore, New light on the new age, *Skeptical Inquirer* 13 (3) (1989), pp. 226–40.

[5] I. C. Jackson, *Honor in Science* (New Haven, CT: Sigma Xi, 1986; http://www.sigmaxi.org/)

[6] J. C. Bailar III, Science, statistics, and deception, *Annals of Internal Medicine* 104 (1986), pp. 259–60.

[7] *Maintaining the Integrity of Scholarship* (Ann Arbor, MI: University of Michigan, Office of the Vice President for Academic Affairs, 1984).

[8] E. J. Huth, Irresponsible authorship and wasteful publication, *Annals of Internal Medicine* 104 (1986), pp. 257–59.

[9] *Integrity and Misconduct in Research—Report of the Commission on Research Integrity* (Report to the Secretary of Health and Human Services, the House Committee on Commerce, and the Senate Committee on Labor and Human Resources) (Bethesda, MD: U.S. Department of Health and Human Services, Public Health Service, 1995).

[10] J. Gaston, Another sociological perspective on deviance in science, in *The Dark Side of Science: Proceedings of the Annual Meeting of the Pacific Division, American Association for the Advancement of Science*, B. K. Kilbourne and M. T. Kilbourne, eds. (Washington, D.C.: U.S. Department of Education, 1983), pp. 54–64.

[11] A. C. Higgins, The games of science, in *The Dark Side of Science: Proceedings of the Annual Meeting of the Pacific Division, American Association for the Advancement of Science*, B. K. Kilbourne and M. T. Kilbourne, eds. (Washington, D.C.: U.S. Department of Education, 1983), pp. 10–26.

[12] C. J. Sindermann, *The Joy of Science—Excellence and Its Rewards* (New York: Plenum, 1985).

[13] W. Broad and N. Wade, *Betrayers of the Truth* (New York: Simon & Schuster, 1982).

[14] W. J. Broad, Frauds from 1960 to the present: Bad apples or a bad barrel?, in *The Dark Side of Science: Proceedings of the Annual Meeting of the Pacific Division, American Association for the Advancement of Science*, B. K. Kilbourne and M. T. Kilbourne, eds. (Washington, D.C.: U.S. Department of Education, 1983), pp. 27–34.

[15] Committee on the Conduct of Science, National Academy of Science, *On Being a Scientist*, 2nd ed. (Washington, D.C.: National Academy Press, 1995).

[16] D. J. Miller and M. Herson, eds., *Research Fraud in the Behavioral and Biomedical Sciences* (New York: John Wiley and Sons, 1992).

[17] Responsibilities of awardee and applicant institutions for dealing with and reporting possible misconduct in research, *Federal Register* 54 (151) (1989), pp. 32446–51.

[18] *Misconduct in Research Policy* (Pullman, WA: Washington State University, 1989); http://www.wsu.edu/Faculty_Senate/facmanual.html

[19] J. P. Swazey, K. S. Louis, and M. S. Anderson, University policies and ethical issues in research and graduate education: Highlights of the CGS deans' survey, *Council of Graduate Schools Communicator* 22 (1989), pp. 1–2.

[20] J. P. Swazey, M. S. Anderson, and K. S. Lewis, Ethical problems in academic research, *American Scientist* 81 (1993), pp. 542–53.

[21] *AAAS Member Opinion Poll—Summary Report of Key Findings—Scientific Ethics and Responsibility* (Washington, D.C.: AAAS, 1992).

[22] *Office of Research Integrity Annual Report 1994*, Department of Health and Human Services, Public Health Service, Office of the Assistant Secretary for Health (Washington, D.C.: U.S. Government Printing Office, no. 394-070/30408, 1995).

[23] *Literary Market Place* (New York: Bowker, 1988).

[24] *Science and Engineering Ethics* (Guidford, Surrey, U.K.: Opragen Publications, Volume 1, 1995).

[25] M. J. Zigmond and B. A. Fischer, Programs to Enhance Professional Development web site (Pittsburgh, PA: University of Pittsburgh); http://www.pitt.edu/~survival/homepg.html

[26] L. Buscaglia, *Living, Loving and Learning* (New York: Fawcett Columbine, 1982).

7 | LIBRARY AND LITERATURE WORK

Until modern times, the evolution of life on the planet—including humans—was driven by our ability to cope with and exploit the energy and natural resources around us: to adapt to the environment, create tools, and perpetuate the species. In the future, the ability to navigate and use information will be the hallmark and future of humankind.

—James Burke

Literature work is important to the growth of scholars and researchers. Without reading, library, and information management skills, one cannot develop the writing talents that are crucial to experimental work.

Reading

Reading helps researchers by:

- stimulating ideas
- improving and organizing knowledge
- avoiding duplication of previously accomplished work
- reinforcing or refuting hypotheses

Reading also influences commitments. According to Bogardus, the renowned American naturalist Luther Burbank "based his whole natural world on a new foundation" after reading Darwin. Burbank described his reading experience as "the turning point in my life work."[1] I remember one student whose decision to pursue graduate work in pharmaceutical chemistry was made after reading an early edition of Adrian Albert's *Selective Toxicity*.[2]

Reading also helps develop self-esteem by improving capabilities and confirming difficulties experienced by others. As reading habits become stronger, perspectives develop that improve abilities to contribute to research and its attendant discussions. This promotes respect from peers and causes an inner sense of accomplishment. Once committed to reading, one should seek ways to improve the abilities to search, evaluate, organize, and keep up with the literature.

Library and Information Management Skills

Library and information management have been vastly improved by computer-based catalogs, computerized databases, and on-line and Internet resources and awareness systems that were unavailable just a few years ago. Libraries and librarians remain integral players in education and training and in facilitating the use of these services, but a time is rapidly approaching when graduate students will have access to most library and information resources through a laboratory- or office-based workstation. Even if that time approaches more rapidly than we imagine, it is important to understand the infrastructure—both people and units—that support such services. It is also important to organize approaches to information management skills.

Searching the Literature

There are few ideas that have not already occurred in some way to researchers. Even wholly novel ideas have their parallels in the literature. Before starting an investigation, therefore, it is important to know about previous findings. During subsequent experimental work, literature searches will help uncover information that may help to explain observations and confirm or refute hypotheses. The searches may be simple or complex; they may or may not involve extensive use of computerized systems. Complex searches may require the use of libraries and consultations with librarians.

Using the Library

The word *library* has roots in the Latin "liber," for book. Libraries, however, are more than mere collections of books. They are depositories for many types of materials, gateways to electronic information, and they are instructional centers (see Table 7-1). Universities employ librarians who are willing and able to help researchers with the most complex problems. Indeed, some library professionals recommend that researchers choose a librarian just as they would choose an advisor. It is important, however, to have knowledge of the systems for cataloging and retrieving information.

Many universities have a handbook on library services for faculty and students. The handbook may be available on-line or accessed through the library's homepage on the www. The handbook may have

Table 7-1. Materials Owned and Accessible Through University Libraries

Main Group	Items
Books: general collection[a]	Fiction
	Nonfiction: textbooks, monographs (books written on a single topic), biographies and autobiographies
Periodicals and newspapers[b]	Current issues
	Past issues[c]
Reference books[b]	Atlases (books containing maps, tables, charts, or plates), annual reviews, dictionaries and encyclopedias, handbooks, periodical and abstracting indexes
	Local, state, and federal publications
Special collections[b]	Rare books and manuscripts, and archival materials (e.g., photographs)
Audiovisual and computer-based materials[b]	Compact disc read-only memory (CD-ROM) systems and databases
	Pictures and maps
	Slides, filmstrips, motion picture films, videotapes
	Microfilms,[d] microcards,[e] microfiche[f]
	Networking and hookups to on-line databases
	CD-ROM and other audiodiscs, tape, and cassette recordings
	Globes, models, and specimens[g]

[a] Circulating material.

[b] Noncirculating or limited circulating materials.

[c] Volumes bound or on microfilm reels, cassettes, microcards, microfiche, or CD-ROM.

[d] Reels of 35- or 16-mm film with contents of journals or out-of-print books. Requires a special viewing machine.

[e] Opaque cards with microprint. Requires a different viewer than that used for viewing microfilms or microfiches.

[f] Card-sized sheet of film containing many images. An entire issue of a journal may be published on a single microfiche, which must be read with a special viewer.

[g] Historically important artifacts.

Adapted with modifications from D. N. Dutta, *Libraries and Their Use* (Calcutta, India: World Press Private, 1975), pp. 21, 70–74.

a map describing the type and location of libraries on campus. Having located or accessed a copy of the handbook, identify the main graduate library. Librarians in this facility organize tours and specialized seminars, including discipline-specific presentations that will help with the use of campus materials and services.

Practically every university offers on-line access to the library catalog that lists holdings for the entire campus. Additionally, the on-line capability will extend to literature search databases either directly or through an umbrella searching system such as FirstSearch (On-line Computer Library Center [OCLC], Inc., Dublin, OH), which offers entrée to *Books in Print* and 60 databases covering many fields.

On-line catalogs should be accessible through an office or laboratory workstation. In some institutions, particularly those that are state-supported, on-line catalogs may include links to holdings of several universities. If this pertains to your situation, it will be important to find out how cross-institutional materials are accessed. It is not uncommon in such situations for researchers to have access to reprints of periodical articles electronically, through fax, or overnight mail services.

On-line catalogs offer entry points or modes of searching, which typically include:

- title keywords
- call numbers
- subject keywords
- series keywords
- publisher keywords
- corporate author keywords
- keywords from conference proceedings

Standard subject headings are listed in the *Library of Congress— Subject Headings.*[3] This source was commonly used for choosing terms to begin a search. However, librarians now suggest that key search terms be obtained through "subject headings" found in relevant articles and books accessible on-line or in the library.

Books and periodicals located through the use of the on-line catalog are usually cataloged and shelved according to the Library of Congress or Dewey decimal system. Medical libraries may use a classification scheme developed by the Library of Medicine. Accordingly, periodicals may also be shelved alphabetically by title. The advantage of most classification systems is that books are grouped according to subject. Thus, if a particular title is sought and found to be checked out, other titles of interest will be found nearby or by browsing the on-line catalog.

A lack of on-line entries for a particular topic indicates no holdings in the library. This does not mean, however, that no books exist on the topic. It may simply mean that the library lacks books in this area. To locate relevant books unavailable through your university's library, you might consult bibliographic listings such as *Books in Print,*[4] *Encyclopedia of Physical Sciences and Engineering Information Sources,*[5] *Medical and Health Care Books and Serials in Print,*[6] *Sources of Information in the Social Sciences: A Guide to the Literature,*[7] and *Information Sources in Science and Technology,*[8] some of which may be on-line or accessible through FirstSearch. Books discovered by this process may be available through multi-institutional consortia or inter-institutional loan arrangements that can be accessed with the help of a librarian.

Another rich source of secondary materials is the Internet and the WWW via an appropriate browser (e.g., Netscape) and search engines (e.g., Alta Vista,™ Yahoo!™). It should be noted, however, that there is much ill-documented and incorrect information on the Web and imprimaturs of universities, governmental agencies, or professional societies should be considered as authenticating mechanisms for WWW-sourced materials.

Recent books and other secondary sources may be a good start for a literature search. Literature work in an area new to a researcher, however, will usually require starting at a more fundamental level. This can be done through scientific encyclopedias, dictionaries, and handbooks as listed in literature guides[7-13] or equivalent sites, which may also be accessible on-line through your university library's homepage.

Another way to begin a literature search is to find a good recent review article. The semiannual *Index to Scientific Reviews: An International Interdisciplinary Index to the Review Literature of Science, Medicine, Agriculture, Technology, and the Behavioral Sciences*[14] can be used to locate one or more of the tens of thousands of review articles published yearly. Review journals and annuals are also available in most disciplines (e.g., the Medical Reviews section of *Medline*), and they can be located through the on-line catalog. The potential worth of reviews can be determined by using the following criteria:

- Is the author an acknowledged expert?
- Are the scope and purpose stated clearly?
- How many years are covered?
- Are references up to date?
- Does the author critically evaluate published material?

- Is the review well organized?
- Does the author suggest possible future directions for the re-search being reviewed?

Searching the Periodical Literature

Few literature searches are complete without a search of the periodical literature. The on-line catalog will provide leads to jour-nals that publish articles in particular fields. Finding articles on spe-cific topics will require a search of one or more standard indexes, typically through a computer-based search, perhaps beginning with FirstSearch or equivalent umbrella-type system but continuing with one or more of dozens of specific on-line searching systems (e.g., *Biological Abstracts, Chemical Abstracts*). The on-line search routines may be augmented by in-library use of CD-ROM systems or library-provided access to these systems through your office or laboratory workstation.

Before tackling the periodical literature, consider whether an exhaustive or a narrow search is needed. Are references needed only in English, or must literature in all languages be found? What period of time must the search cover? These are important questions if a com-puterized search is contemplated, because only a few databases cover literature before 1970. After considering these points, decide on the indexes and computer-based systems that are necessary.

Once the topic for the search has been chosen, develop a list of related terms and keywords. As the search is conducted, be open to new terms or phrases that are encountered. Also, be aware of terms that may have been used in earlier indexing but dropped later. Date the previously developed keyword list and add dates to new terms or phrases as the search proceeds.

A bibliographic reference consists of the title of the paper, name(s) of author(s), title of the journal or book, volume and page numbers of the article, and the date. *Biological Abstracts, Chemical Abstracts, Index Medicus,* and other standard "abstracts" are used similarly, and directions for their uses, including lists of periodicals abstracted (with abbreviations), are given in volumes found in the library or through the library's homepage.

A periodical search should begin with the most recently indexed material and proceed backwards. As the search continues, remember to break occasionally to review some of the literature found in the search. This helps to alleviate the tedium of searching. Also, the in-termittent reading may lead to important references through biblio-graphic citations.

Beginning graduate researchers have a tendency to think that all literature searches are exhaustive. Actually, there are many types of searches. Some are aimed simply at finding a specific fact or precedent for an experimental result; other searches are extensive. With experience, researchers develop the intuition of a detective, and they use a combination of traditional searching routines and selective forays into the literature, and on-line and www sources to uncover needed information. The experienced researcher also learns to associate particular types of research with specific researchers around the world. This is the basis for the usefulness of *Science Citation Index* (SCI), which is described in Table 7-2.

Even researchers unfamiliar with scientists in a particular field can use SCI to search backward or forward for citations to a key researcher's work. This novel searching method can lead to quick answers to specific questions. SCI is also useful in reviewing the contributions of researchers and the quality of journals; however, it is conceded that SCI is oriented to first-author citation. Nevertheless, the best researchers are cited often. Also, it is generally recognized that publication in prestigious journals favors citation.

FirstSearch and other standard search systems can be used to locate original research reports, review articles, and abstracts of U.S. and some foreign patents. Full U.S. patents can be reviewed at one of many libraries in the United States that have been listed by Maizell.[12]

Computer-based searches work through the iterative development of search terms and phrases that involve the linking and coordination of terms based on the developing success of the search. These searches also work through Boolean logic and operators such as **AND**, **OR**, and **NOT**, which aid in narrowing "hits." A trivial example might be a nuclear physicist who wishes to search for references containing information on "fusion" **OR** "cold fusion" but **NOT** "fission."

Librarian-assisted on-line searches may be helpful not only in producing search results but in learning routines for searches. With experience, however, researchers (so-called end-users) will readily learn how to conduct their own on-line searches and reserve only the most complex challenges for librarian-assisted or librarian-conducted searches.

The end-user on-line search is typically conducted using the same services and databases as those employed by librarians. At most universities, these services are available gratis through on-line services accessible via library, office, or laboratory workstations. Absent this possibility, commercial services are available, including SciFinder (from

Table 7-2. *Science Citation Index* and Its Use

Subindex	Description and Use
Source Index[a,b]	Alphabetically arranged author index with entries including names of all authors; language code; full paper title; book number (book titles listed in separate section) or journal name, volume, and issue; inclusive page numbers; year of publication; number of references listed in work; and full mailing address of first author.
Citation Index[a]	Alphabetically arranged first-author index with entries including author and abbreviated citation that has been cited during previous year; abbreviated citations including first authors and their works, which cite author's work listed. Full citations of author cited and authors citing work are available through *Source Index*.
Permuterm Subject Index[a]	Significant terms and combinations from titles of works published during year covered with author references. Relevant works are found through first author's name in *Source Index*.

[a] Issued annually and containing references to more than 500,000 papers and other editorial items covered in *Science Citation Index*.

[b] Also contains an index that permits location of authors by their organizational affiliation, and a section for locating anonymously authored papers through publications in which they are cited.

Chemical Abstracts Service) and KR ScienceBase (through the product ResearchStation, from Knight-Ridder), which offer access to databases through desktop workstations and other features such as novel search routines (e.g., commencing searches through concepts and two-dimensional chemical structures).[15] The end-user on-line search using a commercial product may require a password and clearance for search charges, which will be encumbered on a personal, departmental, or research account.

End-user searches of CD-ROM systems can usually be conducted free of charge but may require in-library use. However, as noted previously, many library-based CD-ROMs are now accessible through office or laboratory workstations.

CD-ROM systems are easy to use and allow searches using Boolean operators. Additionally, information obtained through CD-ROM systems (e.g., reference citations and abstracts) can be printed directly or downloaded into databases developed through personal information management software packages (see below), which is also useful in storing and retrieving evaluations of the literature.

Evaluating the Literature

It is important to maximize the benefit of reading research papers. This can be accomplished in several ways.

Writing in science is compact—it is composed of short phrases and sentences. This requires thoughtful reading—digestion of all words. As noted in Chapter 5, time must be taken to examine the quality of experimental work, to ponder hypotheses and conclusions, and to contemplate the need for further experimentation. Speed-reading is useful in scanning journals or abstracts for items of interest, but slow, methodical reading is necessary for serious study.

One's memory is improved by coordinating self-imposed reading assignments with progress in research. Information needs should be anticipated by planning experiments as far ahead as possible and by developing reading schedules. An understanding of the literature also improves during the preparation of reports and papers. Deadlines for writing projects create some "dither," which seems to improve one's ability to learn.

Reading effectiveness is also improved by note taking. This can be done in several ways. For personally owned books, selective highlighting or underlining is useful to emphasize important words or sentences. I also like to write in margins and to catalog the notes in order of appearance on the end papers at the front of the book. Notes and highlights may remain captive within the covers of personally owned books, or the composite information may be keyed or transferred into a personal information database along with notes and literature references obtained from library books, journals, and articles found on-line.

Various software packages are available to develop personal information management systems. These systems have been reviewed by Lundeen,[16] and Tenopir and Lundeen,[17] who have written a book on the design and creation of personal databases using microcomputers. Briefly, personal information management software allows creation of databases containing a blend of literature references, personal notes, excerpts from the literature, and slides, much of which can be imported directly from on-line or CD-ROM databases; all information can be retrieved selectively.

Some personal information-management software packages allow importation of references from current awareness services, the export or sharing of database segments, and the formatting of reference citations to match the requirements of various journals. Thus, a customized management system can be created that facilitates immensely the use of the literature. These management systems also assist researchers in keeping up with the literature.

Keeping Up With the Literature

Millions of books and articles are published in scientific fields each year. Furthermore, the rates of publication in all fields have accelerated during the last few decades, and few library specialists see any change in this trend.

How do researchers keep up with even a small segment of their area of research? How do they simultaneously develop broad perspectives of their discipline and related disciplines? Meeting these seemingly opposite objectives takes planning and commitment. The commitment may require 10 to 20 hours per week for the master's or doctoral student devoted exclusively to thesis or dissertation research. The planning involves an analysis of your literature needs.

Current awareness needs can be divided into:

- professional literature
- general scientific literature
- specialized literature

Professional literature includes information on the activities of members of a discipline and will be found in magazines and newsletters published by scientific societies.[18] The general scientific literature includes journals and books in one's discipline but not necessarily relevant to one's research. Specialized literature includes reports and monographs with direct relevance to one's research. The relative commitments to these three types of literature will vary as one progresses through a graduate career. For example, the general scientific demands of beginning graduate students are large because of the need to pass core courses and to prepare for candidacy examinations. As students progress in their programs, an awareness of specialized literature has to increase to meet developing commitments to thesis or dissertation research. Furthermore, an early naiveté regarding professional affairs will have to be replaced by increasing awareness if one is to be successful in securing a position after graduation.

Now the question may arise, "How do I implement a current awareness program?" This can be done by:

- systematic reviews of on-line databases and library holdings
- using a current awareness publication (e.g., *Current Contents*) or service, which is often available on-line
- using current awareness software (e.g., *Current Contents on Diskette*, *Reference Update*) and transferring that information to a personal information-management system
- joining journal clubs and professional societies
- attending lectures and professional meetings

Review of Library Holdings

Established researchers love the library. They feel at home within its walls or working through library-provided services. This affection comes from habits that should begin during a graduate career. An hour or two should be set aside each week to browse through newly received journals and books. This habit is reinforced by dedicating the same time slot each week.

Current Awareness Publications and Services

One way to review recent contents of most journals in a field is to scan *Current Contents* (Institute for Scientific Information, Philadelphia, PA). This set of weekly publications contains compilations of the contents pages of journals in the following areas:

- agriculture, biology, and environmental sciences
- arts and humanities
- clinical medicine
- engineering, technology, and applied sciences
- life sciences
- physical, chemical, and earth sciences
- social and behavioral sciences

Each issue has a subject and author index complete with addresses of authors designated to receive inquiries and reprint requests. *Current Contents* is also available on-line and should be accessible through your university's library.

Inquiries and requests for reprints of articles from authors is an old tradition in science. In earlier times, this was commonly done by sending a postcard to the author with a description of the article or information desired. Today, through the use of e-mail and the WWW, many researchers have shifted to new modes of inquiry. As noted by the prominent chemist-physicist Thomas George, "Articles in many cases can be brought up on-line and scientists communicate directly with each other electronically rather than by snail mail, including the transfer of technical manuscripts (LaTex has been a big help in this), and we are increasingly keeping more information on the computer."[19]

Besides *Current Contents*, there are several commercial current awareness services (see Table 7-3) that will provide periodic printouts of citations from journals on topics dictated by subscribers, selected sections of indexes, or diskettes with references in prescribed areas, all provided to subscribers by mail for a fee. The diskettes allow for downloading of references into personal information management systems. Weekly or monthly search services are also available for many of the indices. Librarians and an advisor should be consulted about subscription to an apparently desirable service. All of the services require a significant financial commitment, which would have to be approved by an advisor or department chairperson.

Reprint Storage and Retrieval

Students today have to deal with far more information during their graduate careers than did students in previous generations. It is important, therefore, to have a system for the storage and retrieval of notes and reprints from journals. Merely alphabetizing materials according to title and storing them in a box or drawer may be adequate for the items necessary for a single report or publication. The use of such a system for storage of all materials required during a graduate career, however, will lead to hours of frustration when attempting to retrieve information.

Systems should be devised for filing and locating notes and reprints, possibly using one of the personal information management software packages available commercially, and as noted earlier.

Journal Clubs

Participation in journal clubs is an enjoyable way of reviewing literature with friends and colleagues. The groups, developed informally, can gather for one- to two-hour meetings every week or two to

Table 7-3. Examples of Commercially Available Current Awareness Services

Service	Description	Vendor
Automatic Subject Citation ALERT® (ASCA) and ASCATOPICS®	Search services providing weekly reports on articles published in a specific field. ASCA allows more narrow focusing for searches.	Institute for Scientific Information, Philadelphia, PA
BIOISIS	Search services for *Biological Abstracts*. Free booklets and free courses on how to use computer services. BIOISIS/CA *Selects*: 23 separate titles, each on very specific subjects, issued bi-weekly, from the current literature.	BIOISIS, Philadelphia, PA
Chemical Abstracts	Search services for *Chemical Abstracts*. Mailings of selected sections of *Chemical Abstracts/CA Selects*: 133 separate titles, each on specific topics, issued bi-weekly, from the current literature.	Chemical Abstracts Service, Columbus, OH
Excerpta Medica	Search services, on-line and off-line retrieval.	Excerpta Medica, Lawrenceville, NJ
Medline	Search services, on-line and off-line retrieval.	
PsycINFO	Computerized search services.	American Psychological Association, Washington, D.C.

discuss journal articles. The group should have a discussion leader at each meeting who is responsible for reviewing the article(s) in depth. Journal club meetings can be scheduled to include lunch periods, and participants can be encouraged to bring a bag lunch.

Professional Societies

Professionals need societies and associations to promote their welfare and to provide opportunities for continuing education. Prestigious professional societies in relevant disciplines should be identified early in one's graduate career. An advisor may be helpful in choosing one or two organizations that have provisions for student membership (membership fees for students are often significantly less than regular membership fees). After joining, regular mailings of newsletters, magazines, and other periodic notices will be received, which will help improve one's familiarity with an associated profession. The mailings will also provide information on forthcoming meetings.

Lectures and Professional Meetings

Universities are visited frequently by traveling scholars and scientists. Most university departments schedule seminars for visiting scientists during the academic year, and it is wise to select lectures of interest to attend.

Information on departmental seminars is available through campus publications and university web sites, which typically have "calendar of events" hyperlinks.

One should take advantage of opportunities to hear noted scientists in fields of interest. The lectures will often be informative and inspiring since many researchers discuss the failures and difficulties they have experienced in their work.

Attending professional meetings is important for presentation of scientific papers and for making contacts that may be useful when seeking permanent employment. Besides satisfying these needs, professional meetings give life to the literature. Meetings provide opportunities to hear and visit with scientists whose papers have been read. Opportunities may also exist to visit with representatives of instrument manufacturers, publishers, and other information service organizations. These are worthwhile activities, and it is important to discuss with an advisor the possibilities of attending regional and national meetings during one's graduate career.

Becoming a good researcher is dependent on developing skills for searching, evaluating, and keeping up with the literature. These skills are essential for three of the most important jobs of the researcher: writing, presenting, and publishing papers, and preparing theses and dissertations. These topics are discussed in the following three chapters.

References

1 E. S. Bogardus, *Leaders and Leadership* (New York: Appleton-Century, 1934).

2 A. Albert, *Selective Toxicity*, 2nd ed. (New York: Wiley, 1960).

3 *Library of Congress—Subject Headings* (Washington, D.C.: Library of Congress, 1996).

4 *Books in Print*, Authors Vols. 1–4, Titles Vols. 5–8, and Publishers Vol. 9 (New York: Bowker, 1996–97).

5 M. A. Smith, D. A. Wilt, and J. B. Erickson, eds., *Encyclopedia of Physical Sciences and Engineering Information Sources*, 2nd ed. (Detroit: Gales, 1997).

6 *Medical and Health Care Books and Serials in Print*, Vols. 1 and 2 (New York: Bowker, 1995).

7 W. H. Webb, *Sources of Information in the Social Sciences: A Guide to the Literature*, 3rd ed. (Chicago: American Library Association, 1986).

8 C. D. Hunt, *Information Sources in Science and Technology*, 2nd ed. (Englewood, CO: Libraries Unlimited, 1994).

9 E. B. Davis, *Using the Biological Literature: A Practical Guide* (New York: Dekker, 1995).

10 H. R. Malinowsky, *Reference Sources in Science, Engineering, Medicine and Agriculture* (Phoenix: Oryx Press, 1994).

11 F. W. Roper and J. A. Boorkman, *Introduction to Reference Sources in the Health Sciences* (Chicago: Medical Library Association, 1994).

12 E. Mount and B. Kovacs, *Using Science and Technology Information Sources* (Phoenix: Oryx Press, 1991).

13 For Government Publications, see Government Publications Office (GPO), available through FirstSearch or the www: http://www.access.gpo.gov/. The GPO database goes back to 1976 and is updated monthly.

14 *Index to Scientific Reviews: An International Interdisciplinary Index to the Review Literature of Science, Medicine, Agriculture, Technology, and the Behavioral Sciences* (Philadelphia: Institute for Scientific Information, 1972–95).

15 J. H. Krieger, Chemical research faces opportunities, challenges from information tools, *Chemical and Engineering News* 73 (13) (March 27, 1995), pp. 26–41.

16 G. Lundeen, Software for managing personal files, *Database* 12 (3) (1989), pp. 36–48.

17 C. Tenopir and G. Lundeen, *Managing Your Information: How to Design and Create a Textual Database on Your Microcomputer* (New York: Neal-Schuman, 1988).

18 P. D. Dresser, ed., and A. L. Enrich, assoc. ed., *Scientific and Technical Organizations and Agencies Directory*, 3rd ed., Vols. 1 and 2 (Detroit: Gale, 1994).

19 Personal communication, T. F. George, Chancellor/Professor of Chemistry and Physics, Office of the Chancellor, 213 Old Main, University of Wisconsin–Stevens Point, Stevens Point, WI 54481-3897; http://www.uwsp.edu/admin/chancell

8 | WRITING SKILLS

"You should say what you mean," the March Hare went on. "I do," Alice hastily replied; "at least—at least I mean what I say—that's the same thing, you know."

"Not the same thing a bit!" said the Hatter. "Why you might just as well say that 'I see what I eat' is the same thing as 'I eat what I see'!"

—Lewis Carroll, *Alice in Wonderland*

Writing spans the sublime to the ridiculous. All researchers must write. It is therefore important to develop approaches and styles that ease the task. Success in graduate school and advancement in a professional career depend on one's writing abilities.

Students should begin early in their graduate careers to improve writing skills. Improvement requires an understanding of the elements of good writing, methods for improving writing skills, and tips on writing specific pieces, from memos to book reviews.

Elements of Good Writing

Fielden[1] noted that good writing is characterized by four elements:

1. Thought
2. Correctness
3. Appropriateness
4. Readability

Thought

Well-written pieces are thoughtful. Passages are well organized and faithful to the stated purpose of the work. Good writing contains proper hypotheses, assumptions, and conclusions. It shows a lack of bias and portrays believable justifications. Thoughtful writing reflects the author's enthusiasm and persuasiveness when needed (e.g., correspondence, grant proposals, and reports).

Correctness

Good writing contains correct grammar, punctuation, and spelling. Correct writing is coherent. It is marked by proper syntax and good sentence transitions. Correct writing is neat. It contains judiciously chosen headings and subdivisions.

Appropriateness

Good writing has the right tone. The reader is neither patronized nor buried in verbosity and pompousness. Appropriate writing gives the reader a clear idea of needs and desires.

Readability

Good writing is readable. It flows smoothly. It does not require the rereading of every other sentence. Readable pieces have a lead-off topic sentence followed by sentences that outline the work. The reader knows early where the material is heading and how the work will turn out. Readable works contain logically presented ideas. These works also have clear transitions from paragraph to paragraph. Summarizing statements appear periodically to help the reader understand prior text.

Approaches to Good Writing

There are many books available on writing nonfiction, and researchers will find it useful to read at least one of them. Two of my favorites are the books by Day[2] and Zinsser.[3]

Good writing, like all creative activities, develops with practice and a willingness to try new methods. One method that is essential for the modern researcher is word processing. In subsequent sections, allusions will be made to this skill and its attendant equipment. It is up to researchers to choose the hardware and software that they find most suitable.

Choosing software for word processing should be based on a set of criteria that includes reliability, ease of use, and compatibility with other software programs (e.g., spreadsheet and database filing). To facilitate communications, it is also useful to consider compatibility of software with that used by colleagues, faculty, and staff in your program or department.

Regardless of the choices of hardware and software, most people find that an outline is a good place to begin writing efforts. Once an outline has been developed, it is useful to write against a self-imposed deadline. If the introductory section of a paper is started at 9 a.m., for example, see if it can be finished by noon. The "dither," or tension, generated by the deadline helps the creative process.

Preparing Notes and Outlines

Different writing efforts require different degrees of planning. Major writing tasks, such as papers and dissertations, require review of books, papers, research notebooks, and reports. The notebooks should contain notes and conclusions reached at the time of experimentation. Reports written for an advisor or for a granting agency should be prepared to allow direct transfer of sections to manuscripts. This "makes things count double."

Once references and notes have been organized, an outline should be prepared. Researchers may use topic or sentence outlines, or a combination of both. Some people like to prepare a "very rough draft," which serves as a basis for their outline. Others like to use an annotated outline containing reference notations and topic sentences. Regardless of the approach, the writing efforts will be assisted by a word processor that permits facile changes and transfer and deletion of text from one section to another, or from one document to another. Word processing software should also contain a spell- and grammar-check, synonym finder, and functions for creating tables.

After the outline is complete, consider having it reviewed by an advisor and friends. It is a good idea to develop a "writing friends" system for review of outlines, reports, and manuscripts. Find one or two friends who write well. Make a pact with them to review one another's work. This arrangement can be immensely helpful during one's graduate career.

Try different approaches for the preparation of outlines. Remember that there is no right or wrong way. Find the method that works well for you.

Write, Rewrite, and Rewrite

Red Smith, the Pulitzer Prize–winning sportswriter, noted, "Writing is easy. You just sit at the typewriter, open a vein, and read it out a drop at a time."[4] All professionals know that writing is difficult, but the best way to start is to start. Words on the screen "fuel" further efforts. Follow an outline. Try beginning with a topic sentence (it is better to make it more general than not) and follow with some sentences that outline the paragraphs to come. The actual act of writing will help the creative process. As words appear on a computer screen, new ideas will emerge.

Write simply. Stick to subject-verb-object sentences. Avoid long, beginning adjectival phrases that the reader is forced to remember before coming to the subject of the sentence.

Keep most sentences under 40 words. Produce contiguous sentences of varying lengths. Include summary sentences at the end of major sections. Once the writing has begun, try to compose as much as possible without stopping. Worry about revision later.

Try using the outline like a To Do List. After completing an emotionally exhausting section, reward yourself with a soft drink, a fresh cup of coffee or tea, or a walk around the room. This allows time to reflect on accomplishments and to encourage subsequent efforts. Use headings liberally. One accepted format is:

MAIN HEADING

Main Subheading
  Text begins here . . .

  Secondary subheading. Text begins here . . .

Use the active voice rather than the passive voice where possible. Try to inform rather than impress. Some people have a tendency to try to sound important. Others' faults are verbosity and excessive use of jargon. These failings also lead to problems with syntax.

Jargon includes confused, strange, technical, obscure, and often pretentious language. Technical words must be used in scientific writing, but they should be properly defined. All other forms of jargon should be avoided (e.g., "at this point in time" for "now," and "in a number of cases" for "some," as noted in Day[2]).

With practice, writing styles can be improved. Booth suggests writing as though you are talking to the reader.[5] The "talk" must be grammatically correct and devoid of colloquialisms. This approach is aided by consciously trying to speak well. The training includes speaking slowly, choosing words deliberately, and finishing each sentence. Other approaches to writing styles are described by Zinsser[3] and Strunk and White.[6]

Revision is an indispensable part of writing that is facilitated by a word processor. Indeed, word processors have made inadequate revision of written works inexcusable.

Good authors revise their works five or more times. The revision process provides the best opportunity to clarify thoughts and to correct possible contradictions. Try to develop empathy for the reader. Keep asking, "Could I understand this material if I were reading it for the first time?" You might also try thinking of how the work would appear to a reader whose native tongue is not English.

During the revision process, try to cut out wordiness. The clutter is minimized by eliminating adjectives and adverbs as much as possible. We overuse words such as "very," "quite," "rather," "fairly," "relatively," "several," and "much." In English, nouns may be used to modify nouns. These noun adjectives (e.g., gas engine, monoamine oxidase, life science) are useful but can become confusing if stacked (e.g., albino mouse liver monoamine oxidase).

There are different approaches to the revision process. Tichy recommends "cooling" or allowing a piece to sit for a day or longer before revision.[7] Some writers wait a week. This helps you see work as others will see it. It is often surprising how confusing complex sentences or phrases seem after they have "cooled off" for a few days.

A second revision process, recommended by Mullins,[8] calls for section rewriting:

1. Write the first section and leave it alone.
2. Revise the first section before writing the second section.
3. Revise the first and second sections before writing the third section.
4. Etc.

The Mullins method works best if a work is completed in six sections or less. Otherwise, unnecessary repetition is introduced before the last section is written.

A third method for revision involves reading passages aloud. This helps uncover awkward and confusing sentences.

Regardless of the method used, the revision process should be done slowly and repeatedly until you are satisfied. The final revised work should be reviewed by an advisor and "writing friends." Ask for a tough review, and respond constructively.

Writing Tools

The tools of a good writer include dictionaries, synonym finders, specialized handbooks, and grammar and composition guides. *Webster's Third New International Dictionary*,[9] *Webster's New Collegiate Dictionary*,[10] and the *Random House Dictionary*[11] have been recommended for scientists. A *Roget's Thesaurus*[12] or its software equivalent is invaluable. Additionally, it is useful to have a personal copy of a science dictionary such as the *Larousse Dictionary of Science and Technology*.[13] Related works such as *Scientific English: A Guide for Scientists and Other Professionals*, will also be useful.[14]

A guide to English usage and grammar should be obtained. Several of these are available, such as the works by Fowler[15] and Ebbitt.[16] The question may now arise, "How will I afford all these books?" Fortunately, many of the basic writing tools are available on the www.[17] The other references may be available in the laboratory or study area for graduate students in an advisor's group. Research grants provide funds for the purchase of books. If the reference books cited are not available, an advisor may be persuaded to buy some with his or her grant funds. University libraries will also have the reference works cited.

Notes, Memoranda, and Letters

Communications include written and e-mail notes, memoranda, and letters. I differentiate between notes and memoranda. Notes are informal messages. Memoranda are more formal than notes, and they are reserved for correspondence between persons within the university. Letters are the most formal type of correspondence.

All types of correspondence are now commonly sent by e-mail, because of its ease, cost, and speed. However, the tone of e-mail correspondence should be modulated according to the formality suggested by the situation.

Written notes should be dated and contain the full name of the recipient. Here is an example of a format for written notes:

Joseph Procter
12-29-98

Joe,

    Your books are ready at the printer.

Bob

Memoranda can be written using this format:

To:
From:
Re:

The "Re" alerts the recipient to the subject of the memorandum. The body of the memo is developed using the communicator's guide:

- Here's where I am
- Here's how I got there
- Here's what I want from you

Below is an example of a properly constructed memorandum from the chairperson of a human subjects institutional review board to a graduate student researcher.

MEMORANDUM

September 11, 1998

To: Mary Chavez, Department of Psychology
From: Lee Baker, Chair, IRB
Re: IRB Meeting, September 25, 1998

You are invited to attend the IRB meeting scheduled for Friday, September 25, 1998, at 4:00 p.m. in the Main Building, Room 6.204.

Our IRB regularly meets with investigators whose proposals are being considered for approval. We hope that you can be present at our meeting to answer questions about your proposal, "Depression in Sensory-Deprived Subjects." Thank you for your cooperation.

This memorandum is direct, yet courteous. It fulfills the goals of the communicator's guide and gives enough information for the recipient to respond correctly.

A format for business letters is:

Your address
Date

Title, name, position,
and address of recipient

Re: (optional)

Salutation: (colon or comma)

Body of letter.

Complimentary close,

Your signature

Your name typed
and your position
Enclosures: (list them)

Your initials in capital letters followed by / or : and the initials of the typist in lowercase letters

The intended recipient of the letter should be addressed properly. If he or she has an earned doctorate, "Dr." can be used or the initials of the highest earned degree can be placed after the recipient's name (e.g., Joseph G. Cannon, Ph.D.; Elaine S. Waller, Pharm. D.). Faculty may be addressed as "Prof." (or "Professor") if appropriate. It is better to address non-doctoral professorial faculty as "Professor" rather than "Ms." or "Mr."

Be sensitive to national customs and individual preferences. In some countries (e.g., Germany, Switzerland) it is common to refer to male doctoral faculty as "Dr. Prof." or "Herr Dr. Prof."; women faculty would analogously be referred to as "Dr. Prof." or "Frau Dr. Prof." Some women prefer "Mrs." or "Miss" to "Ms.," and they will indicate this in their correspondence. Retired deans and professors may correctly be referred to as "Dean" and "Professor," respectively.

The titles of recipients' positions should be added after their names (e.g., Howard B. Lassman, Ph.D., Director of Clinical Pharmacology; Catherine R. Stimpson, Ph.D., Editor). This is proper protocol for all professional administrators. The remainder of the address should be complete, and it may contain accepted abbreviations (e.g., Co. for Company, Inc. for Incorporated).

The "Re" is useful in citing important numerical notations. Manuscripts considered for publication have number assignments that should be referred to in correspondence containing revisions. Letters referring to orders for merchandise should include purchase order numbers (e.g., Re: Order no. 27,632A).

The salutation should read "Dear Dr." ("Prof.," "Ms.," "Mr.," etc.) followed by a colon. A colon is proper when the recipient is not known well. First names followed by a comma can be used for friends. When no specific person is addressed, "Dear Sir/Madam" can be used. Other salutations include "Dear Person" or "Dear People," or "Dear" followed by a word denoting the person's profession. A letter to a pharmacist, for example, might include the salutation, "Dear Pharmacist (surname)." Analogous salutations can be constructed for accountants, architects, dentists, engineers, nurses, etc.

The body of the letter is developed by using the communicator's guide. Letters are often longer than memos but should be restricted to one page if possible. Necessary details can be included in appendices that should be properly labeled to prevent loss.

The tone of letters should vary according to their purpose. Most Americans welcome informality. Other nationalities tend to be more formal, except between friends. Try to strike a balance between stuffiness, which is unbecoming, and casualness, which may be insulting.

The complimentary close may read "Yours truly," "Yours faithfully," or "Yours sincerely." Some prefer a simple "Sincerely."

Persuasiveness

Memos, letters, and prospective sections of reports and grant proposals may require persuasion. There are strategies for being persuasive. It is important to understand that being persuasive does not mean being a huckster or one prone to hyperbole. Assertions must be based on fact. Arguments should be developed logically. Sensational claims or examples should be avoided. Ewing suggested that if you have a sympathetic reader, arguments can be ordered with the strongest appearing last.[18] Lead off with the strongest argument if the reader is unsympathetic.

Try appealing to positions held by the individual or institution. A university or industrial firm committed to excellence in research will be affected positively by arguments for policy changes that elevate standards.

Copies of memos or letters can be used to one's benefit. A copy judiciously sent (i.e., as indicated by a "c," "ec" [electronic copy], or "pc" [photocopy; "cc" for carbon copy is an anachronism], and the recipient's name in the lower left-hand corner of the letter) to an official higher than the recipient can be a useful power play.

Be cautious with power plays. They should only be used as a last resort. A complaint to a professor about his or her performance in a course, written with a pc to the department chairperson, can backfire. Misunderstandings can create ill feelings and cause repercussions later. Honest dialogue is better than confrontation.

Students sometimes harbor a fantasy that begins with their righteous correction of a professor's errors during a lecture or seminar. This act is met with thunderous applause from the class and a humbling of the professor. This is stuff best left to Hollywood. A rational approach is more often effective. Confidential memos or letters call for honest dialogue. If this doesn't work, the "copy tactic" can be used.

Research Notebooks

The research notebook is used to prepare a record of experimental work. It is also the repository for diagrams, graphs, and standardization routines that permit repetition of experiments. A research notebook should be bound with stiff covers and may have loose-leaf pages. Its pages should be consecutively numbered, and the book should contain a table of contents, preferably at the beginning.

Copies of all notebook entries (possibly produced on a word processor) should be prepared and stored in a safe place. Loss of notes through fire or other accidents can be catastrophic.

Notebook descriptions should include:

1. Title, date, and purpose
2. List of required equipment and materials
3. Outline of procedures, including calibrations and standardizations
4. Observations and data
5. Graphical representations of data
6. Equations, calculations, and statistical tests
7. Records of unusual events that may influence results
8. Conclusions
9. Modified hypotheses and plans for future experiments
10. Researcher's signature

If an experiment resembles a previous one, page references may be substituted for items 2 and 3. Data should be collected on data sheets specifically designed for the experiment or created through the table-preparation functions of word processing software (e.g., Microsoft® Word). Such software or equivalent spreadsheet software (e.g., Microsoft® Excel) also allows automatic mathematical conversion of columnar data to graphic displays. The computer-developed tabular data or spreadsheets should be affixed to notebook pages when experiments are complete. Data should not be recorded on loose scraps of paper that can be lost. Also, sections of the notebook should not be rewritten because errors can be made during transcription of data.

Notebook entries end with conclusions and descriptions of unusual events that may have influenced the results. Conclusions should be analyzed in terms of experimental hypotheses. If necessary, alternative hypotheses and experiments should be proposed. Completed notebook entries should be signed and the signature of a witness added if there are plans to apply for a patent.

Notebooks should be kept up-to-date. Entries should be made as close as possible to conclusions of experiments. Otherwise, errors may occur or motivation for notebook updating may wane. As noted earlier, a common temptation is to forget negative results and not enter them in the notebook. This can lead to unnecessary embarrassment and duplication of work.

The research notebook is an important part of research. However, it is not useful in conveying results to others. This activity requires a report.

Reports

Report writing is an integral part of research. Paradis noted that the preparation of reports and related pieces (e.g., research articles) requires as much as one-third of the time of professionals who choose a career in research.[19] If a career is chosen in a highly regulated industry (e.g., pharmaceuticals) or in government, the requirement for report writing will increase.

Reports should answer the following questions:

- What are you trying to do?
- Do the methods and conclusions make sense?
- What is the importance of the work?

Report-writing skills are beneficial throughout a graduate career. The practice gained in writing reports will also help in the preparation of research articles, grant proposals, and the thesis or dissertation. The importance of report writing makes it imperative that a research advisor be chosen who regularly requires this activity. A good advisor will also prepare timely critiques of work. This encourages students to gain the necessary writing experience.

Report writing helps to clarify one's thoughts about research. John Stuart Mill noted, "Hardly any original thoughts on mental or social subjects ever make their way among mankind, or assume their proper importance in the minds even of their inventors, until aptly selected words and phrases have, as it were, nailed them down and held them fast."[20]

Reports are useful at three stages of research: at the beginning, during difficulties, and at project's end. During the development of a research project, the report should include:

1. A statement of the problem and underlying hypotheses
2. Analysis of how the problem developed
3. Description of possible solutions
4. Steps to be used to implement preferred solutions
5. Costs

Intervening reports help researchers confront anomalies in data, plan new experiments, and modify hypotheses. As noted by Beveridge, "The systematic arrangement of the data often discloses flaws in the reasoning, or alternative lines of thought which have been missed.

Assumptions and conclusions at first accepted as 'obvious' may even prove indefensible when set down clearly and examined critically."[21] Final reports serve as preludes to manuscripts for publication.

Report Format and Style

Here is a good format for interim and final research reports:

- Title
- Table of Contents
- Abstract
- Introduction
- Experimental Section
- Results
- Discussion
- Bibliography
- Appendices

The title page contains the full title and name(s) of the author(s), department, and university. Titles should indicate the subject and scope of the report. Avoid unnecessary words in the title such as "Investigations of," "Interesting Aspects of," and "Results of." Develop a title that is a label rather than a sentence. Use noun adjectives and correct syntax. Do not use abbreviations, chemical formulae, proprietary names, or jargon in a title. Ask these questions about the title: How will it look as a title to a paper? Does it entice the reader into the rest of the report?

The title page should bear the date of the report and a serial number if this is the practice in your department. Do not number the title page. Its imaginary number is "i" if the report has a table of contents. If the report is short and contains no table of contents, then the title page bears an imaginary "1."

A table of contents is useful for reports longer than 10 pages. It can be composed of headings and subheadings from the body of the report and their corresponding page numbers. Subheadings are indented from headings and may be used selectively. Try to keep the length of the table of contents to one page. If it is longer, number continuing pages "iii," "iv," etc. The table of contents and subsequent sections are numbered in the lower center of each page.

The abstract is the most important part of the report. It is the section most people read, and it gives readers an overview of the report. The abstract, therefore, should be written last and with special care. Here are the sections of the abstract and sources of material for each:

- Statement of the problem—"Introduction"
- Brief description of methodology—"Materials and Methods"
- Main Findings—"Results"
- Conclusions—"Discussion"

The abstract should be written simply. Use the past tense, write in the third person, and minimize the use of technical language. Include only ideas and claims found in the report. The abstract of a report describing a new method should contain the method's basic principles, range of operation, and degrees of accuracy and precision.

Abstracts should not include references to tables and figures, descriptions of published work, or reference citations. Conclude the abstract with one or two major points from the discussion.

Some people begin reports by writing the experimental and results sections first. Others begin by writing the introduction, which should be started with a statement of the problem. Continue development of the introduction with background information, and add reference citations using the Harvard system (see below). Previous work should be surveyed, but not in an encyclopedic way. It is not necessary to cite every known reference. The introduction should contain a brief review of the material presented in the report. This helps the reader decide whether it is worth continuing. Introductions should be interesting and should inspire further reading.

The experimental section contains descriptions of experiments and methods. Include enough details to permit repetition of the experiments, but omit procedures already reported. Develop the experimental section in a sensible order. Don't be afraid to deviate from the chronology of the experimental work. A research report should not read like a diary. Rather, experiments should be arranged logically to benefit the reader.

Use headings to highlight paragraphs describing materials, equipment, methods, and experiments. The materials and equipment listings should include sources and manufacturers, respectively. Give technical specifications and purities of reference chemicals and materials. Provide accurate identifications of animals, plants, and microorganisms, including genera, species, and strains. Animals should also be described by weight, age, sex, and special handling. Experimental sections for human subjects research should include selection criteria and details of informed consent procedures.

Descriptions of methods and experiments should also contain the *what*, *where*, *when*, and *how* of procedures. Use abbreviations and a format approved by the journal that will probably publish the work.

Do not repeat published procedures, but do cite germane references. If the published method is complex, give a two- or three-sentence description of it, using an introduction such as "The method of Day (10) was used. Briefly, it involved. . . ." This brief description helps the reader develop a conceptual understanding of the results without having to consult another paper.

The results section can be written after the introduction or experimental sections. Describe the results in the past tense using the chronology established in the previously prepared section(s). Do not repeat material from the experimental section. The experimental section is a description of *what was done*. The results section helps to describe *what happened*.

Tables should be prepared to stand alone. The reader should be able to make sense of a table without reading the entire report. This is accomplished through clear titles and headings, and well-developed footnotes. Column headings can be abbreviated and should contain units of measurements. Columns containing descriptive material and independent variables should appear on the left. Columns for dependent variables go on the right. Table 8-1 is an example of a well-constructed table. Note how like elements are read down. Compare the format of Table 8-1 with that of Table 8-2. The cross listing of the like elements in Table 8-2 makes it more difficult to comprehend. Number tables consecutively and refer to them in numerical order in the results section.

Table 8-1. A Well-Constructed Table Showing the Characteristics of Fruit-Bearing Plants of North America[a]

Plant	Average Growing Season (mo)[b]	Average Height (cm)[c]	Color of Fruit	Average Yield of Fruit (kg/plant)[c]
Grapefruit	4.2	400	Yellow	170
Lemon	5.6	300	Yellow	30.0
Lime	5.2	275	Green	25.5
Strawberry	8.0	5.75	Red	0.090
Tomato	9.2	180	Red	5.00

[a] Bogus data
[b] In South Texas
[c] During the growing season

Table 8-2. A Poorly Constructed Table Showing the Characteristics of Fruit-Bearing Plants of North America[a]

Determination	Grapefruit	Lemon	Lime	Strawberry	Tomato
Avg. growing season (mo.)[b]	4.2	5.6	5.2	8.0	9.2
Avg. height (cm.)[c]	400	300	275	5.75	180
Color of fruit	Yellow	Yellow	Green	Red	Red
Avg. yield of fruit (kg./plant)[c]	170	30.0	25.5	0.090	5.00

[a] Bogus data
[b] In South Texas
[c] During the growing season

Day refers to graphs as pictorial tables.[2] Tables help with the listing of data, and graphs help depict trends in data. Graphs are useful in planning experiments and should be used liberally in reports prepared for an advisor.

The graphic displays and analyses are facilitated by the use of word processing or spreadsheet software as noted above.

The discussion is written after the results. It should not, however, recapitulate the results. Continue to write in the active voice when appropriate. Put the results in context with published work. Use the past tense when referring to your results and the present tense for published results. Until work has been subjected to peer review and published, it should be considered tentative. In contrast, published work is accepted. Avoid anthropomorphic expressions such as "the results suggest . . . ," "the instruments measured . . . ," and "the data point to . . . ." Results, instruments, and data are capable of such feats only in cartoons.

Discuss the theoretical and practical importance of the work, and include the possible implications of failures experienced. Remember that you cannot prove negatives. As noted by Sagan, "Absence of evidence is not evidence of absence."[22] Confront ambiguities and apparent contradictions in the work. When choosing between hypotheses, consider the admonition of the great anthropologist Loren Eiseley, who noted that scientists must "flourish Occam's razor and reduce hypotheses about a complex world to human proportions."[23] Stated differently, scientists prefer the simplest explanation that agrees with all the evidence. Also, be careful not to introduce into the discussion observations that were not covered in the results. Limit speculation; assess the importance of the findings on the basis of previously published work.

The discussion section should conclude with plans for the near future (i.e., the next two to six weeks). Give a brief description of what experiments will be done and indicate expected results. Suggest how these results might affect current hypotheses. Indicate any problems or special needs that can be anticipated during the planned experiments.

The bibliography should be prepared in the format of the journal that may publish the work. Journals use three bibliographic systems:

- Harvard system
- Citation order
- Alphabet-number system

The Harvard system involves the use of a surname notation for citing references in the text. The reports of Ryan (1996) and Ryan and Okita (1994) are referred to with names and dates (in parentheses) as indicated, or as follows: "Gene transfer techniques have been evaluated (Ryan 1996; Ryan and Okita 1994) in. . . ." Citations with three authors appear as "Ryan, Okita, and Cook (1995)" the first time they are cited, and as "Ryan et al. (1995)" or "(Ryan et al. 1995)" subsequently. The last two formats are used uniformly for references having four or more authors. When there are two or more "Ryan (1996)" references, the first one cited becomes "Ryan (1996a)" and the second becomes "Ryan (1996b)." The reference list is compiled alphabetically for the bibliography. References such as "Ryan 1996a," "Ryan 1996b," and "Ryan 1997" are arranged chronologically and alphabetically.

The Harvard system helps during writing and revision. Citations can be noted in the developing text without stopping to type out the reference. The name citations are used later to prepare the complete bibliography.

The citation order system uses a series of numbers starting with "1" to identify references. Number assignments follow the order of appearance of references in the report. The bibliography lists the references in numerical order.

The alphabet-number system is similar to the Harvard system, which is often used during the writing process and in compiling the reference list. Subsequent use of the alphabet-number system requires numbering of the alphabetized reference list. The numbers are then substituted for the author-date entries in the report. Numbers are used parenthetically or as superscripts depending on the format of the journal that may publish the work.

The references in a report should be checked against the original literature. Make sure that each reference is accurately cited. Do the references contain the material claimed? Are the names, dates, and volume and page numbers correct? This is a tedious process, but references "locked into" a report will save time during subsequent writing efforts.

A common system of abbreviations has been developed by the American National Standards Institute[24] for journal title words, as indicated by Day.[2] These abbreviations should be used uniformly except for one-word journal titles (e.g., *Science*, *Biochemistry*), which are unabbreviated. Abbreviations of words like "arachnology" (spiders), "entomology" (insects), and "ichthyology" (fish) always end after the "ol." The standard abbreviations are used with the volume-page number-year format of the journal in which you intend to publish.

Quotations require special care. All words and punctuation marks must be checked to ensure that they are correct. Split quotes "are denoted by three dots . . . as indicated." Check for proper placement and use of diacritical marks (such as the two dots of the umlaut) in foreign words.

Appendices containing supplementary data may be added following the bibliography. Number them sequentially, and use title and column headings similar to those in tables. Detailed instructions for routine procedures (sometimes referred to as standard operating procedures, or SOPs) can be included as appendices to monthly research reports. Copies of the SOPs can be posted in the laboratory or other work areas for daily use. Write-ups for computer routines, animal care procedures, and screening protocols for human subjects research are also good appendix materials. There should be a feeling of pride when your first research report is completed. Later, the value of reports will be realized during the development of research papers and your thesis or dissertation.

Research Papers

There are several types of research papers. The four most common are:

- articles or full-length papers
- notes
- communications
- letters

Articles are written to describe extensive and definitive studies. The format and style of articles are similar to those of research reports. The elements of research reports are listed in Table 8-3 along with modifications that are necessary to prepare articles. The recommendations are general and given as guidance. Before preparing any research paper, check the "instructions to authors" found periodically in journals. The text material for research papers is often distilled from several research reports, and word processors help in the preparation of composite material.

Table 8-3. Recommendations for Converting Research Reports into Research Articles

Format Element of Research Report	Changes Needed to Prepare Research Article
Title page	Add key words for literature retrieval system.[a]
Abstract	Statements may require numbering depending on journal.
Table of contents	Omit.
Experimental section	May use tables to list large numbers of research specimens (e.g., plants, animals).
Results	Avoid presentation of negative results.
Discussion	Limit speculation, discussion of negative results, and plans for future research.
————	Add summary and conclusion sections as required by journal.
————	Add acknowledgment section to express gratitude to funding sources,[b] faculty, students, and staff.
Bibliography	Note reference system used by journal.
Appendices	Omit.

[a] Check journal instructions for relevance and limitations.
[b] Include grant numbers when relevant.

Footnotes can support statements that do not fit easily into the results and discussion sections. Some journals require the use of footnotes for proprietary and manufacturers' names. Footnotes can also be used to respond to criticisms of reviewers, but they should not be overused. Twedt refers to their overuse as "footnoteitis."[25] Symptoms of "footnoteitis" are observed when at least half of the text manuscript pages are devoted to footnotes.

Tables and graphs require special attention when papers are prepared for publication. The number of tables and graphs should be limited. Find ways of incorporating mean data into the text. If tables are needed, use the guidelines described under research reports.

Graphs are known as line drawings to printers, and they must be prepared carefully, using word processor, appropriate software, and a laser printer. Photos (with dimensions recommended by the journal) of graphs, rather than original graphs, may be prepared and submitted for publication. Write your name lightly in pencil on the back of each photograph, making sure the imprint does not show on the front of the photograph.

Figure legends are usually typed on separate pages. Include enough information in the legend to permit the figure to stand alone. A key for different curves must be included, e.g., sheer-stress as a function of temperature: carbon steel (-o-), vanadium steel (-X-), and iron (-Δ-).

Black-and-white photographs or micrographs can be used for figures. Alternatively, color photographs can be used, but the resulting images are not distinct. The cost of so-called halftone work may be very high, and this cost is often passed on to the authors. In some research, however, a picture is worth a thousand words and the cost of photographic illustrations is justified. For example, multicolor molecular graphics representations obtained through computer visualizations are commonly observed in the literature.

Expert help should be obtained in preparing clear photographs. If the subject matter is a set of small objects (e.g., micrographs of colonies of microorganisms), crop the photograph to accentuate the set. Arrows, numbers, or letters can be placed at key points on the photograph through the use of press-ons available from art supply stores. Be sure to identify the added symbols, numbers, or letters in the figure legend. Write your name or all the authors' surnames lightly in pencil on the back of each photograph and micrograph. Also with pencil, mark the top of each photograph with an arrow.

Watch the numbering of tables and figures. Many journals use Roman numerals for tables and Arabic numerals for figures. Find out if the word "Figure" can be abbreviated in the text and figure legends. Write in the words "Table" and "Figure," with appropriate numbers, in the margins to indicate points in the text where tables and figures should appear in the published paper. Use blue pencil if the paper is to be directly photoreproduced.

Notes, communications, and letters differ in purpose and style from research articles. Notes are used to describe definitive, though shorter, studies than those presented in articles. Some journals dispense with abstracts in notes; otherwise, the format for notes is the same as that of articles.

Communications and letters are short (i.e., less than five typewritten pages) papers of unusual importance. Manuscripts prepared as communications are rarely divided into formal sections. Rather, the text contains elements from the introductory, experimental, results, and discussion sections. The brevity of communications and letters requires a minimum of figures and tables. The figures and tables that are included, however, must be accompanied by experimental detail. Examples of well-prepared figures and tables can be found in issues of the journals *Nature* and *Science*.

Research papers should be word processed according to the "instructions to authors" in the journal of choice. This typically involves production of 12-point type, double-spaced printing on 22 × 28-centimeter paper with 2.5- to 3.5-centimeter margins. Use a laser printer and number each page, starting with page two.

Book Reviews

It may be rare for graduate students in some disciplines to prepare book reviews for publication. Book reviews, however, are commonly prepared by graduate professionals. Thus, it is helpful to gain the necessary experience during an academic career, perhaps through joint reviews with an advisor—an activity that would be particularly appropriate for this book.

Book reviews are solicited by journal editors who supply a gratis copy of the book for review. The following evaluations will be expected:

- The range and nature of the book
- Whether or not the book meets the author's stated purpose
- How the book fits into a field or discipline
- The appropriateness of the references cited

- How the book compares with other published works
- The themes or theses developed by the author
- Typographical and grammatical errors
- The style and accuracy of the text

Keep the criticisms objective and constructive. Avoid personal attacks even if you know and dislike the author. Remember that scholars and their work will be remembered long after the work of critics.

Briefly review the background and credentials of the author. This is most important in the social sciences. Hammett noted that the approaches of scholars such as historians and sociologists are often influenced by the personal situation of the author.[26]

Be aware of the length requirement established by the journal for the review. Follow format guidelines carefully, and supply necessary ancillary information such as biographical data on the author(s).

Few graduate students write books during their academic careers. Thus, some may find it difficult to develop the empathy necessary to review others' books. However, once students have begun writing their theses or dissertations, they begin to understand the rigors of producing book-length works. Guidelines for preparing theses and dissertations are contained in the next chapter.

References

[1] J. Fielden, What do you mean I can't write?, *Harvard Business Review* May–June (1966), pp. 144–56.

[2] R. A. Day, *How to Write and Publish a Scientific Paper*, 4th ed. (Phoenix: Oryx Press, 1994).

[3] W. K. Zinsser, *On Writing Well: An Informal Guide to Writing Nonfiction*, 4th ed. (New York: HarperCollins, 1990).

[4] R. Smith, interview (Washington, D.C.: National Public Radio, June 1986).

[5] V. Booth, *Communicating in Science: Writing a Scientific Paper and Speaking at Meetings*, 2nd ed. (New York: Cambridge University Press, 1993).

[6] W. Strunk, Jr., and E. B. White, *The Elements of Style* (New York: Macmillan, 1959).

[7] H. J. Tichy, *Effective Writing for Engineers—Managers—Scientists* (New York: Wiley, 1966).

[8] C. J. Mullins, *A Guide to Writing and Publishing in the Social and Behavioral Sciences* (New York: Wiley, 1983).

[9] *Webster's Third New International Dictionary of the English Language, Unabridged*, P. B. Gove, ed.-in-chief (Springfield, MA: Merriam-Webster, 1993).

[10] *Webster's Ninth New Collegiate Dictionary* (Springfield, MA: Merriam-Webster, 1989).

[11] *Random House Dictionary of the English Language*, 2nd ed., S. B. Flexner, ed.-in-chief (New York: Random House, 1987).

[12] *Roget's II: The New Thesaurus*, 3rd ed. (Boston: Houghton Mifflin Co., 1995).

[13] *Larousse Dictionary of Science and Technology*, P. M. B. Walker, general ed. (New York: Larousse, 1995).

[14] R. A. Day, *Scientific English: A Guide for Scientists and Other Professionals*, 2nd ed. (Phoenix: Oryx Press, 1995).

[15] H. W. Fowler, *Dictionary of Modern English Usage*, 2nd ed., E. Gowers, ed. (New York: Oxford University Press, 1965).

[16] W. R. Ebbitt, *Writer's Guide and Index to English*, 6th ed. (Glenview, IL: Foresman, 1978).

[17] Teachers.Net Reference Desk (Santa Monica, CA: Teachers.Net, current); http://www.teachers.net/library/refdesk.html

[18] D. W. Ewing, *Writing for Results in Business, Government, the Sciences, the Professions*, 2nd ed. (New York: Wiley, 1979).

[19] J. C. Paradis, Improving technical communications to improve productivity, *Chemical and Engineering News* 61 (11) (1983), pp. 31–32.

[20] J. S. Mill, *A System of Logic*, 8th ed. (New York: Harper, 1891).

[21] W. I. B. Beveridge, *The Art of Scientific Investigation*, rev. ed. (New York: Norton, 1957).

[22] C. Sagan, *The Dragons of Eden* (New York: Ballantine Books, 1977).

[23] L. Eiseley, *All the Strange Hours—The Excavation of a Life* (New York: Charles Scribner's Sons, 1975).

[24] *American National Standard for Writing Abstracts*, ANSI Z39.5-1979 (New York: American National Standards Institute, Inc., 1979).

[25] D. W. Twedt, A marketing strategy for marketing knowledge—Or, how to publish and prosper, *Journal of Marketing* 69 (April 1977), pp. 69–72.

[26] H. B. Hammett, How to write a book review: A guide for students, *Social Science* 65 (1974), pp. 263–65.

9 PREPARING THESES AND DISSERTATIONS

Nearly all the successful writers I have known had to make the dissertation close to an obsession.

—David Sternberg

Most research master's degree and all Ph.D. degree programs require original contributions to research that are documented in a thesis or dissertation. The thesis or dissertation requirement can be anticipated with anxiety, or steps can be taken to prepare for it and ease the task. Several books have been written that include guidelines for the preparation of dissertations.[1-4] It is useful to review suggestions made by authors of these works, and to consider approaches and methods that can be instituted early in a graduate career to lessen the difficulty of meeting thesis or dissertation requirements.

Planning and Approaches

The ways in which theses and dissertations have been written are probably as numerous as the resulting documents; however, three general methods are prevalent:

1. *Late preparation method:* Begin writing when all the research is complete.
2. *Composite method:* Combine two or three major research papers.
3. *Hierarchical method:* Develop several writing projects throughout the graduate career that become the basis for the thesis or dissertation.

The first method includes preparation of a dissertation proposal and research summaries, but the major writing task is left to the last several months of graduate work. For most researchers, the late preparation method can be a source of frustration and an almost overwhelming fear of the "final writing task." This fear may be exacerbated by delays caused by inadequate analysis and summarization of research results near the expected end of the graduate career. The tension escalates as the research notebooks get thicker and more numerous. Finally mounted, the writing effort commences with trepidation. Clearly, the late preparation method is not recommended.

A second method of thesis or dissertation preparation involves the joining of two or more full-length research papers through appropriate introductory and transition sections. Assuming prior publication of two formidable research articles, a "composite" document might be envisioned as follows:

1. Chapter 1—Introduction containing historical background
2. Chapter 2—First full-length research paper
3. Chapter 3—Bridge section containing descriptions of how research papers 1 and 2 are connected
4. Chapter 4—Second full-length research paper
5. Chapter 5—Overall summary, conclusions, and description of potential areas for new research

The composite method is popular in laboratory-based sciences. It requires special effort to ensure coherence in the final product. However, it may save time compared to more traditional approaches, and the method almost assures that one or more publications will result from the thesis or dissertation. The composite method may not be acceptable in all departments and graduate schools. Also, the composite method may be opposed by faculty members who are asked to serve on a thesis or dissertation committee. Thus, consensus on the method should be sought in the early stages of a dissertation project.

One additional aspect of the composite method requires attention. The papers that are melded into a composite-method dissertation are likely to have multiple authors. Accordingly, you should indicate in the introduction or transition chapters the portions of the published research that are most closely associated with your efforts.

The third, or hierarchical, method for thesis or dissertation preparation requires planning and coordination of writing activities throughout one's graduate program. Doctoral students, for example, encounter the following writing assignments during their graduate careers:

1. Dissertation and grant proposals
2. Research reports
3. Term papers for courses
4. Research papers
5. Written candidacy reports and proposals
6. Dissertation

The hierarchical method requires you to dovetail the purposes and objectives of as many of the above assignments as possible. Early planning is essential for this method.

If the hierarchical method is planned, it should be discussed with your advisor as soon as possible. Determine whether departmental or program rules forbid orienting the writing projects as proposed. In some programs, for example, students may not develop a candidacy proposal akin to their doctoral research.

Instructors usually permit a choice of term paper topics in courses as long as the topics are relevant to course objectives. Why not choose topics that will have to be covered in the thesis or dissertation historical review? Additionally, instructors in research methods or scientific writing courses may allow preparation of a thesis or dissertation introduction as a course requirement. Dovetailing course and dissertation objectives is a good way to make things count double.

Dissertation and thesis writing is also eased by a planned approach to experimental work. Experienced researchers relate how they mentally plan tables and figures when designing and conducting experiments. This type of planning helps to keep final thesis or dissertation writing efforts uppermost in one's mind, which increases efficiency.

Use of the hierarchical method should encourage close contact with an advisor. Joint planning efforts will include intermingling purposes of papers, careful review of intervening writing efforts (e.g., research papers), and sharing perceptions of how much work will be necessary to complete the thesis or dissertation research.

Characteristics of Theses and Dissertations

The graduate thesis or dissertation is generally encyclopedic in nature. It contains an extensive survey of the literature, including historical background. The model dissertation is illustrated with diagrams, photographs, and charts. Tables and examples abound, providing broad perspectives on the dissertation subject. A prize-winning dissertation at the University of Texas at Austin (*Dynamics of Huastec Ethnobotany: Resources, Resource Perception and Resource Management*) exemplifies the model dissertation. The work was completed by Janice Alcorn, who lived for more than a year with the Huastec Indians, studying their culture and learning their language. Alcorn's findings included maps of vegetative zones, diagrams of houses and farmsteads, and line drawings of local ethnogeography. The dissertation narrative contained a comprehensive analysis of the ecology, culture, and sociology of Huastec life. A work of immense proportion was produced, which was eventually published as a book.[5] Similar models of excellence should be sought by all writers of theses and dissertations.

Each year the Council of Graduate Schools sponsors a national competition that recognizes authors of exceptional dissertations. Information on these awards can be obtained through any graduate school.

Dissertation Blues

Negative feelings that occur particularly during the research and writing stages of dissertations can be described as dissertation blues.[3] Heading the list of symptoms is the sense of being overwhelmed. This feeling is most prevalent when plans for the dissertation are not developed early in one's program.

Feelings that the wrong project was chosen plague graduate researchers, especially when results do not develop as expected. Commitment and self-assurance are necessary to plod ahead. Encouragement can be found in the work of others. John Sheehan, the first chemist to synthesize penicillin, reflected on the dark days leading up to his success: "No matter how discouraging the laboratory work turned out to be, I simply went back in and tried more approaches. I went back to the library and read more research reports. I thought more about the problem. As long as I could avoid asking myself the defeating question 'Should I really be in this?' I remained immune to the anxieties that accompany scientific research. For me it was always forward march, never halt, never retreat."[6] Commitment like Sheehan's is aided by publication of intermediary results, as noted with the hierarchical method.

Dissertation researchers often have nightmares about their hypotheses being wrong or having left something out of their experiments. Such worries are frequently alleviated by conducting good control experiments. The control experiments may be suggested during the course of experimentation or after experiments have been completed. Patience and perseverance are necessary to follow through with these "post hoc" control experiments and to correct results accordingly.

Writer's block, or the apparent inability to put thoughts on paper, is a common myth about dissertation writers. As indicated in
Chapters 4 and 8, writers need schedules and determination to write
around and through writer's block.

Worries about being scooped are common among dissertation
researchers. These concerns come from the notion that the whole
dissertation project will have to be abandoned if a similar paper appears in print before the completion of the research work. A related
fear is that published work was not picked up in the literature search
before the dissertation project was begun. This latter problem is addressed by searching overlapping databases and reviewing bibliographic
entries in current publications. Most often, earlier thoroughness is
confirmed. Simultaneous publication is common, and it results from
different groups working at the forefront of science. Consolation is
derived from the idea that the literature serves to inform and confirm
results. Furthermore, it would be rare if two researchers approached a
problem with identical methodology. Thus, completed research should
be publishable even if similar results have unknowingly been obtained
elsewhere.

Dissertation blues also includes a feeling of becoming "burned out."
Extended and concentrated efforts create the illusion of losing track of
the world and becoming mentally exhausted. The effect is common
among professionals in many fields. The American writer Alice Adams
noted that she does not work on writing "jobs" as much as they work on
her.[7] Dissertation "jobs" can be similarly captivating, but the work serves
as a prelude to long-term projects that are essential during all professional careers. Just as the athlete needs to work for months or years to
build endurance, the scholar builds perseverance and feelings of self-
worth through the rigors of the dissertation process.

Relations with Thesis and Dissertation Committee Members

Thesis and dissertation committees operate differently in various universities. Sometimes, graduate students have close and continuous relationships with their committees. Other times, students
interact with their committees only during the final stages of the thesis or dissertation research.

The policy on thesis or dissertation committees should be determined early in a graduate career. An active and helpful committee is
desirable, as indicated in Chapter 3. In some cases, it is wise to peti-
tion for a coadvisor if the expertise of a committee member is found
crucial to the thesis or dissertation research.

Students should be sensitive to the expectations of the committee. Interim abstracts and reports should be developed according to the schedule prepared with an advisor. All outlines, abstracts, reports, and thesis or dissertation sections should be reviewed by an advisor before being distributed to committee members.

Approaches to Writing

Guidelines for the preparation of a thesis or dissertation are similar to those described (Chapters 4 and 8) for preparing research papers. The major difference between writing a research paper and writing a thesis or dissertation is the length of time necessary for the latter efforts. Consequently, it is wise to find a suitable space for writing the thesis or dissertation. The space should preferably be near the library and a workstation with entrée to university library holdings. It should be secure enough that books and papers can be left from day to day, and it should preferably be off-limits to family and friends. Try to obtain a space with characteristics as close to these criteria as possible.

Before beginning to write, obtain materials from the graduate school that describe format requirements. Obtain recommendations of good theses or dissertations previously approved by members of your committee. Review these works for ideas on approaches and format. Set a high standard for the work to be written.

Develop a schedule for the thesis or dissertation writing and stick to it. Minimize the influences of friends and family during the writing process. Create an understanding that the writing time is sacred and necessary for "training" as a scholar. Helpful tricks include closing a study door or having a radio on while writing. These actions signal others that you are hard at work.

Deadlines, Word Processing, and Binding

Graduate schools have several deadlines during the term in which a degree is granted. The thesis or dissertation abstract has to be in on one date, the first full copy on another, and copyright forms and the final draft on still another date. The worrisome thing about all of these deadlines is that they generally come early in the term. Thus, it is wise to plan a term before the term of graduation to meet the deadlines.

Regarding typing, I reemphasize that all graduate researchers should become skilled at word processing. If there is some handicap that prevents the development of this skill, then a contract with a typist should be made before the dissertation is begun. Universities employ many secretaries who moonlight. Some graduate-student spouses seek part-time word processing work. Ask around the department for recommendations. Settle on someone who is known to be reliable and who is emotionally stable. Expect a bill of several hundred dollars for typing services for a thesis or dissertation.

Some graduate schools permit submission of theses or dissertations in electronic formats including CD-ROM. Consideration is also being given to WWW dissertations, although all electronic formats raise archival accessibility questions that will require attention before they are widely adopted. Nevertheless, the possibilities are intriguing, including the incorporation of novel sound and visual effects that could be particularly advantageous in certain studies. For example, graduate researchers in speech communications (nonverbal communications) and classical archaeology (ancient Celtic cultures) at the Universities of Texas at Austin and Virginia, respectively, have pursued dissertations via CD-ROM technology.[8] Before proceeding down these novel pathways, however, it will be critical to determine relevant policies at your institution.

As noted earlier, the abstract is one of the first items that must be deposited with a graduate school. Abstracts of theses and dissertations generally have the following components:

1. Introduction
2. Statement of the problem placed in the context of the discipline
3. Underlying hypotheses
4. Methods used
5. Major findings
6. Short discussion of the novelty and importance of findings, and implications for the field of study

Like the abstract of a research paper, the thesis or dissertation abstract can only be written near the end of the thesis or dissertation research. The dissertation abstract should also be prepared with utmost care because of its impact on committee members and people outside the university after its publication in *Dissertation Abstracts*.

A thesis or dissertation can be copyrighted through forms available from the graduate school. As noted earlier, a copyright provides a right of protection or monopoly for a thesis or dissertation for the author's life plus 50 years, and it exists whether or not an application has been filed with the Register of Copyrights. However, as noted by Dolores Marsh of University Microfilms International (UMI, publisher of *Dissertation Abstracts*), a suit for damages for unauthorized use of material will not be successful without an approved copyright.[9] In general, copyrighting is less important for theses or dissertations that will be converted into papers for publication in journals than it is for work that may ultimately be published in a book or for material that may be used in securing a patent on a process or product. But it is important to be aware of copyright regulations, particularly as they apply to borrowed materials (e.g., fair use).[10]

The graduate school is likely to require two or three bound copies of a thesis or dissertation for deposition in university libraries (be sure to check on acceptable modes of copying). Most committee members do not expect bound copies of theses or dissertations although it is nice to present one to an advisor.

Oral Examination

At most universities, a committee must approve a thesis or dissertation before it can be accepted by the graduate school. The review process typically involves a one- to three-hour oral exam that requires careful preparation.

The main reason for the oral defense is to allow the committee to obtain a perspective on the candidate's grasp of the thesis or dissertation and his or her field of study. This perspective is gained through a range of questions that focus on the contents of the thesis or dissertation. The committee may also ask questions in areas of apparent weakness displayed by the candidate during previous research meetings and candidacy exams. Preparation for these questions requires introspection about your work and possible academic shortcomings.

The oral defense is typically an open exam. Departmental faculty and students may be invited to attend the exam by an advisor or department chairperson. Candidates may also invite graduate school friends who might welcome a preview of their fate! Seriously, the exam should not be anticipated in foreboding terms. Indeed, consolation should be derived from two thoughts. First, candidates are more knowledgeable than anyone else about their theses or dissertations. Second, while committee members have to satisfy a commitment to scholarship through questioning, they want to see the candidate succeed. Committee members to varying degrees view a candidate as their student. It is in their interest to see the candidate complete his or her program successfully.

A copy of the thesis or dissertation should be brought to the exam. After greeting the committee members, the committee chairperson or graduate school representative (who may by tradition chair the examination) may ask the candidate to step outside the room for a few minutes. During this time, the committee will briefly review the candidate's academic record and agree to rules for the examination. At the start of the exam, the chairperson may ask the candidate to give a short biographical sketch of herself or himself.

The exam is likely to continue with the candidate being asked to briefly (15 to 20 minutes) review the thesis or dissertation. This review should include an honest appraisal of its strengths and weaknesses. Also, the major contributions and implications of the work should be summarized.

Following the review, the meeting chairperson will signal the beginning of the questioning. In some cases, the chairperson may ask the first question, which can set the tone for the remainder of the exam. However, a chairperson who is also the student's advisor will often relinquish his or her right of first questioning to prevent allegations of directing the course of the exam. Questions are put forth by each committee member successively. The committee members may refer to specific pages in the candidate's thesis or dissertation during the questioning. Some questions will be challenging. In fact, I have known chairpersons who purposely ask committee members to construct tough questions to ensure that the exam ends up as a "memorable experience."

Candidates should not be surprised by questions about their plans for the future and their ideas for publication of the thesis or dissertation. Committee members may also be interested to learn how the candidate thinks the thesis or dissertation contributed to her or his growth as a scholar. Of course, there is often the proverbial question, "If you could remain here a few more years, what problems would you pursue as uncovered by your dissertation?" This question is often ironically asked toward the end of the exam, when the candidate may be near emotional exhaustion.

After each committee member has had a chance to ask questions, the chairperson may call for further questions at random. When the questioning is completed, the chairperson will most likely excuse the candidate but ask him or her to remain nearby. In the candidate's absence, the committee members will discuss the exam and the thesis or dissertation. A vote will be taken on the outcome. Rules on voting procedures and consequences vary among universities, but at minimum, a majority vote will be required for one of the following actions:

1. Unconditional pass with the exception of correction of typographical errors
2. Conditional pass subject to minor revision(s)
3. Conditional pass subject to major revision(s)
4. Failed presentation but passed thesis or dissertation
5. Complete failure

The third outcome may require additional experiments and writing efforts to satisfy the committee. Outcome 4 is unusual and easily prevented through the hierarchical method in which a candidate has developed confidence through previous presentations. Outcome 5 is rare. A complete failure at this stage of a student's career reflects either incompetence on the part of the student and the advisor or is the result of prejudice. In any event, a petitioned review of the student's case would be in order. The decision of a review team as approved by the graduate dean would be final.

In all likelihood, your examination will be successful. The announcement will be received with an extraordinary sense of achievement. Congratulations by each of your committee members will evoke a sense of elation as you formally join the community of advanced scholars and researchers.

The development of research papers and a thesis or dissertation provides opportunities to submit works to journals or book publishers and to present findings at scientific meetings. These activities are discussed in the next chapter.

References

[1] J. G. Calvert, J. N. Pitts, Jr., and G. H. Dorion, *Graduate School in the Sciences: Entrance, Survival, and Careers* (New York: Wiley-Interscience, 1972).

[2] V. M. Sugden, *The Graduate Thesis: The Complete Guide to Planning and Preparation* (New York: Pitman, 1973).

[3] D. Sternberg, *How to Complete and Survive a Doctoral Dissertation* (New York: St. Martin's Press, 1981).

[4] D. Madsen, *Successful Dissertations and Theses* (San Francisco: Jossey-Bass, 1983).

[5] J. B. Alcorn, *Huastec Mayan Ethnobotany* (Austin, TX: University of Texas Press, 1984).

[6] J. C. Sheehan, *The Enchanted Ring: The Untold Story of Penicillin* (Cambridge, MA: MIT Press, 1982).

[7] A. Adams, interview (Washington, D.C.: National Public Radio, February 1989).

[8] K. S. Mangan, Universities wonder whether to allow dissertations on CD-ROM, *Chronicle for Higher Education* 42 (26) (1996), p. A-15.

[9] D. E. Blum, A dean is charged with plagiarizing a dissertation for his book on Muzak, *Chronicle for Higher Education* 35 (35) (1989), p. A-17.

[10] K. D. Crews, *Copyright Law and the Doctoral Dissertation: Guidelines to Your Legal Rights and Responsibilities* (Ann Arbor, MI: UMI, 1992).

10 PRESENTATION AND PUBLICATION OF PAPERS

Scientists, starting as graduate students, are measured primarily not by their dexterity in laboratory manipulation, not by their innate knowledge of either broad or narrow scientific subjects, and certainly not by their wit and charm; they are measured, and become known (or remain unknown), by their publications.

—Robert A. Day

The job of the scientist is to discover, confirm, and communicate new knowledge. As discussed in Chapter 8, writing research papers is a prerequisite to communication, which includes presentations at meetings and publications in books and journals.

Presentation of Papers at Meetings

Presenting papers at meetings is an important part of the research process. Work is better understood after it has been presented before an audience. Also, exposure gained through presentation helps researchers meet colleagues who may become important future contacts.

Besides providing contacts, presentations invite criticism. This allows for new interpretations and changes in research directions. Occasionally, compliments will be received. These promote self-confidence and stimulate personal development. Receiving compliments should also prompt one to compliment other deserving scientists. Heightened sensitivity to others' achievements is essential for personal growth and the development of new friendships. Indeed, few things stimulate conversation better than expressing interest in others' work.

Scientific presentations require planning, and they involve the "art of science." It takes imagination and skill to develop good presentations. It also takes the courage of a performer to present one's work before peers. Fortunately, like the work of the artist, the task is eased with practice.

Submission of Abstracts

A paper must first be "accepted" before it can be presented at a scientific meeting. This requires the submission of an abstract of the work for review by members of the scientific organization that is sponsoring the meeting. The abstract covers work that is complete but unpublished. The previously discussed guidelines for abstract preparation can be used, but there will be strict length and format requirements. Signatures of sponsors may be required on the abstract form. A second, more extensive conference report may have to accompany the abstract.

According to Day, the conference report should omit the "Introduction," "Materials and Methods," "Results," and "Discussion" headings and be written more like a lengthy abstract.[1] The conference report serves as a truly preliminary report. It can include modest speculation, alternative theories, and suggestions for future research. The abstract, conference report, and supporting documents, if any, may have to be submitted six to nine months before the meeting. Thus, the timely submission of abstracts will take planning and attention to detailed instructions supplied by the sponsoring society or association. An advisor is a good source of guidance on meetings and societies in a discipline.

Types of Presentations

Papers are given at scientific meetings as podium or poster presentations. A podium presentation is typically a 15- to 20-minute oral and visual (e.g., slides) description of work. Poster presentations are visual descriptions of work represented on poster boards, which are displayed for hour-long periods. During the viewing period, the author or authors are available to answer questions or explain their work.

Podium Presentations

Podium presentations are often frightening to new scientists who fear going blank or erring before an important audience of scientists. The chance of this happening, however, can be minimized by planning, hard work, and practice.

Preparation of a good podium presentation starts with a written talk or notes. The written material is prepared from an outline and addresses the following questions:

1. Why was the work done?
2. How was the work done?
3. What was found?
4. What do the results mean?
5. How can the results be summarized, and what do they mean for future experiments?

Answering the first two questions should take about one-third of the presentation. The last two-thirds of the talk should be devoted to the remaining questions, with the bulk of time devoted to questions 3 and 4. During the write-up, avoid getting bogged down in details. Stick to the salient aspects of the work. Stress those points that will be most important to the audience. Day recommended that an oral presentation be pitched to a more general audience than would read one's publications.[1] Prepare material that can be covered comfortably in the time allotted.

Presentations in a foreign language should be prepared for verbatim delivery unless one is fluent in the language. Talks in English should not be read. Rather, notes to guide the presentation are prepared in large type (18- to 24-point) with a word processor. The material, typed on index cards or sheets of paper, should be correlated to the slides or other visual aids in the talk—one card or sheet per visual aid.

During the preparation of the presentation outline, ideas for visual aids will emerge. Some of these will include tabular data and figures previously prepared for research reports and papers. As the write-up is revised for the presentation, the functions of visual aids should be considered.

1. *To support the spoken word.* Audience recognition is aided by visual aids depicting necessary jargon (e.g., geologically important crystals, genera and species of plants and animals, names of diseases).
2. *To amplify the spoken word.* Oral descriptions of periodic, patterned, and cyclical events are supplemented by diagrams. A point may also be emphasized metaphorically by a carefully chosen cartoon.
3. *To replace the spoken word.* Certain conditions or phenomena (e.g., weather patterns, topographical features, trends in data) can be understood only through use of pictures, charts, or graphs.

The visual aids may consist of 35 mm (so-called 2 × 2 inch) slides or plates prepared for computerized projection via PowerPoint or equivalent software. Avoid overhead transparencies. Overhead projectors are commonly available but may give neither large nor clear enough images for most meeting rooms. Furthermore, most meeting-room arrangements do not permit simultaneous use of the podium (where notes are placed) and the overhead projector, thus making use of the projector awkward.

Veterans of scientific meetings often tell stories of presentations marred by poor visual aids. Ineffective visual aids contain one or more of the following faults:

- *Clutter.* Too much is included on the visual aid. This confuses listeners who may be unable to decipher or see material.
- *Poor organization.* Visual aids are difficult to understand. Too many ideas are presented at once.
- *Poor contrast.* Visual aids are difficult to read.
- *Distraction.* Visual aids are prepared with an unusual color or too many colors.

Bauer suggested the KISS method for making visual aids: "Keep it simple, stupid!"[2] This brazen charge is meant to emphasize the importance of preparing slides or other visual aids that are the antithesis of those described above. In the case of slides, clutter is prevented by strictly limiting the words on slide plates (sheets containing words, graphs, or other matter to be photographed). This is accomplished by using one of two rectangular templates that can be drawn on a blank sheet of paper. A 9 × 6 inch template should be used to prepare slides containing a maximum of nine lines centered and spaced 1/2 inch apart. The type should be no smaller than 18 point and should be prepared with a word processor and laser printer. Parallel considerations should be given to plates prepared as a part of PowerPoint or equivalent electronically produced visual aids.

For slides, figures and diagrams should be prepared to fit horizontally (preferably) or vertically within the 9 × 6 inch template. Axes of graphs and other printing should be prepared with 18-point type. Use a good laser printer to maximize the black-white contrast. High-contrast printing prevents poor contrast in the resulting slides. For traditional slide preparation, figures or diagrams can be outlined with lines and margins drawn in light-blue pencil. The blue lines will not photograph. Existing graphs or figures can be corrected or altered with white correction fluid and press-on letters and numbers. The final corrected slide plate may appear as a jumble of blue lines and patches of dried correction fluid; however, it should photograph well (as tested by examination of a photocopy of the plate) or may be scanned for use in PowerPoint or equivalent systems.

Graphs from reports or notebooks are reproduced (for slide plates) using a microprocessor and appropriate software (e.g., Microsoft® Excel) or are imported into PowerPoint or equivalent software for production of electronic presentations.

Slide plates should be photographed professionally through a service that may be available on campus. Most university photo services offer choices of slide colors and mounts. So-called diazo slides provide a white image on a colored background. Blue diazo slides, for example, are commonly used and are easier on an audience's eyes than black-on-white or white-on-black slides. Other diazo colors include brown, green, purple, and red. These colors are satisfactory as long as the image is in white. In contrast, slides prepared with colored letters (e.g., red, blue, and green) on a black background may be hard to read when projected.

When preparing PowerPoint or equivalent presentations, consider color and pattern combinations that are soft on the eyes and are not so complex as to detract from the important components of the presentation.

With traditional slides, mounts may be cardboard, plastic, or metal. Before choosing one, examine sample slides prepared by local photo service people. Consider cost and the quality of the mount chosen. Some cardboard and plastic mounts are so flimsy that the film buckles. This can cause annoying unevenness in projected images. You may avoid this problem by mounting film between thin glass sheets, which are subsequently mounted in plastic or metal.

Prepared slides should be viewed with a projector to determine clarity and projected size. Another simple test is to hold a slide at arm's length in front of a light source. If the slide is easily read, it is likely to project well before an audience. If not, larger lettering or different contrasting colors may be needed. Preview PowerPoint or equivalent presentations using projection equipment similar to what will be available at the meeting. One complication here is the myriad of hardware and software options for projection of electronically prepared presentations. Defend against equipment failure by precisely describing your hardware and software needs to the session organizer so that appropriate equipment and hookups (i.e., for a laptop computer) are secured.

Once the notes and slides are complete, practice presentations should be given. Begin by mentally going through the talk several times. Try this during trivial tasks such as bathing, riding public transportation, or waiting for an appointment. When the talk is nearly memorized, ask an advisor and some friends to listen to one or more mock presentations. During the practice presentations try to:

- Speak directly to the listeners and establish eye contact.
- Use notes effectively—do not read from them.
- Vary your tone of voice and watch pronunciation; do not lower your voice at the end of sentences.
- Take time with thought transitions. Try to minimize verbal crutches such as "ah" and "you know." A good way to break this habit is to pause and take a breath through your mouth.
- Display some animation with your body and arms, but avoid needless or repetitive gesturing and pacing.
- Show enthusiasm for your work.

After the practice presentations, solicit comments and questions. The resulting discussions will help you anticipate inquiries that may arise during the meeting presentation.

The presentation should now be ready to debut at a scientific meeting. On the day of the presentation, arrive early at the meeting room to survey lighting, podium placement, and other arrangements. Make sure the slides are loaded properly in the projector or the computer projection equipment is operating correctly. This is the speaker's responsibility even if an audiovisual technician is in charge.

There are some aspects of the actual presentation that cannot be anticipated, including the exact composition of the audience and unavoidable nervousness. These factors should not be allowed to defeat you. Avoid telling the audience that you are nervous or that you feel ill prepared. The listeners came to learn, not to feel sorry for someone.

Begin the talk as practiced. Try not to fidget or adjust your clothing throughout the presentation. Three or four steps can be taken on either side of the podium to break tension and refocus your concentration. If you seem to go blank during the presentation, try not to panic. Walk a couple of steps, take a deep breath through your mouth, and direct your eyes away from the audience as you concentrate. Your train of thought should return quickly. Alternatively, you can glance at a copy of your complete paper with key phrases underlined or highlighted. As a last resort, a sentence or two can be read verbatim from the paper. This is not recommended for routine use, but some people feel less nervous if they have their paper nearby. Remember that the audience has no idea of what you were going to say. If you stumble slightly or forget a few words, no one is going to chastise you. Everyone in the audience was in your shoes at one time, and many will recall that they did a poorer job during their early presentations.

Watch the time carefully during a presentation. If you forget a wristwatch, be aware of clues from the chairperson of the session. Rising motions or worried glances are signals that time has expired. Respect timing lights or buzzers that may be used by the meeting organizers.

When the presentation is finished, thank the audience for their attention and indicate a willingness to answer questions. Repeat questions posed by members of the audience; then answer them honestly and succinctly. If you don't know the answer to a question, or a question addresses something that has not been done, answer forthrightly.

Sometimes, listeners become emotional about points raised by talks. Remember that science requires critical appraisal, and most researchers can be critical of work without getting personal. Thus, criticism should be taken in the spirit of free inquiry. Occasionally, however, a questioner displays poor manners and may become personally abusive. This is uncalled for and should be addressed properly by the session chairperson.

After the question-and-answer period, thank the audience again and return to your seat. Enjoy the exhilaration of having successfully completed a presentation.

Poster Presentations

Poster sessions have been used routinely at scientific meetings in the United States since the early 1970s. They were developed as a way of accommodating greater numbers of papers at meetings. A two-hour poster session, for example, can readily include 25 or more poster presentations, whereas only six or eight podium presentations would fit into the same time period.

The preparation of posters places special responsibility on the author(s). Posters must stand on their own—a story must be told without explanation. Actually, there is an interesting relationship between the quality of a poster and the inquiries it generates. The informative poster will stimulate questions and discussions. A poster that is poorly organized and technically inferior will repel onlookers.

Plan the posters well. Begin by determining from the meeting organizers the size of the poster boards that will be available. Typical boards are 4 × 8 feet. The poster should contain:

1. Title, names of authors, and their affiliation—this is placed on a banner that spans the top of the poster
2. Abstract

3. Plates for:
   a. objectives
   b. methods
   c. results
   d. discussion
   e. conclusions

Arrange the sections so that onlookers can quickly grasp an overall impression of the work.

Poster plates are prepared to meet guidelines discussed under podium presentations. More detail can be added for poster plates, but it is best to keep them as simple as possible. Once the poster plates are made, prepare large-type versions with a microprocessor and a laser printer, or prepare photographic enlargements measuring about 8 × 10 inches. Lettering should result that is no less than 4 to 5 millimeters in height. Lines for graphs and tables should be no less than 2 millimeters wide. The prescribed enlargements should be readable from 8 feet. The title banner can also be made with a word processor or through photographic enlargements, but individual letters should be 3 to 4 inches in height to be readable at 16 feet. Photographic work should be done with high-contrast film. Printing can be on glossy paper, although MacGregor recommended a matte or pearl-surfaced finish to minimize glare.[3] The pearl-surfaced photos are also less prone to curling. Photographs can be mounted on colored construction paper with a non-water-based glue to prevent wrinkling. Glue sticks are convenient for this purpose. Different-colored backings can be used for each section of the poster. This helps to guide the eyes of onlookers.

After all of the poster materials have been prepared, lay them out on the floor and develop an organized and pleasing arrangement for the plates. Ask an advisor and some friends to view the poster and make comments. After settling on an arrangement, photograph it and use the photograph to duplicate the poster at the meeting. While preparing for the meeting, collect items that will be needed for the poster presentation. These include 5/8-inch steel pushpins and a repair/alterations kit consisting of an assortment of press-on letters, a single-edge razor blade, extra pushpins, a black felt-tipped marker, and cellophane tape. Photocopies of an abstract or other relevant materials may be taken to distribute to interested viewers.

On the day of the poster presentation, arrive at least 30 minutes before the scheduled presentation to set up the poster. Be sure to be present with the poster during the appointed times. If there is the option of staying for the entire time the poster is displayed, take it!

The more personal contact with onlookers the better. Indeed, this is probably one of the greatest advantages of poster presentations over podium presentations.

Encourage questions from serious onlookers by offering to give additional information. Display enthusiasm during discussions with visitors. Don't be afraid to greet and visit with friends who drop by, but try not to devote significant blocks of time to chitchat. Also, try to keep discussions at a reasonable sound level.

During the poster session, observe difficulties that some onlookers may have had with the presentation of the work. Take notes on how the next poster presentation might be improved. Remove the poster on time and save the poster materials for use in preparing slides, or figures for publication.

Publication of Papers

Publication customs vary among disciplines. In some disciplines, graduate students seek publication on their own either before or after graduation. For most fields, however, joint publication with advisors and other workers is the rule. Regardless of the practices in your discipline, it is important to understand the publication process, which includes:

1. Selection of a journal and publisher
2. Preparation of the manuscript for publication
3. Submission of the manuscript
4. Response to reviews
5. Handling galley and page proofs
6. Ordering reprints and handling page charges
7. Referring to unpublished work
8. Responding to reprint requests

Selecting Journals and Publishers

There are many journals in most fields of science. A survey of *Current Contents* will lead to many titles. Journals vary in quality, the most respected generally being those that are published by major societies and associations. Nevertheless, there are some very good journals published by university departments and independent publishers.

Researchers' careers get their greatest boosts from publishing in the best journals. The better journals, however, have rejection rates as high as 90 percent, which may cause scientists to shy away from them. This is unfortunate because one or two solid publications in a prestigious journal may be worth as much as five to ten papers in second-rate journals. The lesson for choosing a journal for a manuscript is clear. Select the most prestigious journals, then narrow the choice by considering comparative circulations. Data on circulation are found on the last few pages of the November and December issues of journals, listed in the "Statement of Ownership, Management, and Circulation." Another factor to consider is the cost of publication. Some journals charge $100 or more per page to publish papers. Also, a processing fee of at least $25 may be assessed when the paper is submitted. Acceptance of a paper for publication is not contingent on payment of page charges, but this payment may be expected except under unusual circumstances. Unless an advisor has budgeted for this cost, it is important to consider whether publication in a journal with page charges is worth the cost.

In some fields, it is common to publish dissertations as books, but finding a publisher can be difficult. Many commercial publishing firms avoid dissertation manuscripts because their narrow scope can lead to poor sales and little profit. For this reason, university presses should be considered. Their purpose is the advancement of knowledge rather than profit, and one is more likely to find publishers of dissertation topics from among their ranks. Make a list of possible choices by consulting a directory of university presses that indicates preferences for manuscripts in particular fields.[4] A priority order can be developed based on the prestige of representative universities and their presses.

Preparation of Manuscripts

The purpose, scope, and format of papers for journals are detailed in notices to authors, which are published at least once a year. Use guidelines in the notice to authors as well as those in Chapter 8 to prepare the final draft. If a book-length manuscript is planned, obtain the publisher's handbook (or equivalent) for authors, which will give details on format. If a paper is being prepared for camera-ready copying, the format guidelines will be extensive and must be reviewed carefully before processing the paper.

The question of authorship should be discussed before a final draft of the paper is written. In some fields, it is common for graduate students to publish their thesis or dissertation research alone. Graduate students in most disciplines, however, publish jointly with their advisor and other faculty or students who are significant contributors to the work. Multiple authorship raises the question of whose name will appear first on the manuscript. This is an important question because modern citation, retrieval, and literature-scanning services can attribute disproportionate credit to the first author. In many research groups, first authorship is based on who is credited with the major ideas in the paper and the write-up. Thus, beginning graduate students will assume a second- or third-author status. Advanced graduate students often earn first authorship.

Whether the manuscript is book-length or a two-page communication, care should be taken to make sure that it is neat and free from misspellings and typographical errors. This requires careful reading and rereading by all authors. Editors and reviewers are favorably impressed by neatness and correctness. Attention to these details indicates a feeling for aesthetics and an appreciation of good work.

Submitting Manuscripts to Publishers

Prepare a cover letter to accompany the submission of a manuscript to a publisher. Address the letter to an editor indicated in a notice to authors and include:

1. A statement identifying the contents of the correspondence, e.g., original manuscript plus prescribed number of copies
2. How the paper should be considered, i.e., as an article, note, or communication
3. A statement indicating that the content of the paper has neither been published nor submitted or accepted for publication by another journal
4. Name and address of recipient of future correspondence if different from those of the author of the letter
5. Suggested names (with addresses) of potential reviewers if the paper covers work in a specialized area
6. A simple note of thanks for considering the manuscript

Book-length works should never be sent to publishers without prior approval. If possible, publishers should be visited to discuss projects.

Papers or book-length manuscripts should be bound carefully in manila envelopes and sent by first-class mail to editors. Enclose the prescribed number of copies and include a self-addressed stamped envelope for notice of receipt if this is customary with the publisher. Also, include a voucher for payment of review charges if necessary.

As an alternative to first-class mail, some journals permit electronic transmission of manuscripts. In such cases, conditions for transmission should be followed carefully.

Be sure to retain electronic and photocopy versions of materials sent to the publisher. For multi-author papers it is proper to supply each author with a copy of the material mailed.

Manuscript Reviews

Word that a manuscript has been received and sent out for review by the publisher should be obtained within days (in the case of electronically transmitted manuscripts) to two to three weeks of submission. If no word is received within three weeks, call or write the editorial office to confirm receipt. A report on the review(s) of manuscripts submitted to journals should be received within six to eight weeks. Book-length manuscripts may take 4 to 12 months. Few papers are accepted outright, but a paper might be deemed acceptable with minor changes. Alternatively, the reviewer(s) may raise significant questions about the work that will have to be addressed effectively to prompt reevaluation by the editor(s). This may require considerable revision and reprocessing.

All criticisms of reviewers should be considered seriously and addressed properly during the revision process. The reviews of two or more referees may have notations (e.g., A, B, . . .) that should be referred to in the cover letter. If no notation is given, assign numbers or letters appropriately. In a response, changes should be clearly described by page-paragraph-sentence-number citations, which are given to help the editor or reviewer locate the revised material. This is effectively done by using different-colored ink for underlining or different type faces developed through word processing for new and revised sections of the resubmitted paper. The underlining can be correlated to colors assigned to different reviewers.

Sometimes, footnotes can be used beneficially to respond to reviewer criticism. One author I know uses footnotes such as "One referee suggested that . . ." to describe a reviewer's concern and to lead into a response.

The revised manuscript and a letter outlining revisions should be returned to the editors. Be sure to include in the letter the number assigned by the editor to the manuscript. If the requests for changes are minor and the objections have been satisfactorily addressed, the editor may exercise his or her prerogative to approve publication. Reviewer requests for major revision, however, may prompt the editor to send the revised manuscript to the referee(s) for a second review. The reviewer's advice will then be considered by the editor in making the final decision. The time from resubmission to receipt of word on the manuscript's fate should be no more than four weeks. Take delight in an acceptance. Alternatively, the manuscript may be rejected at this stage or after the first review.

Editors and publishers are receptive to appeals for reconsideration, but rejection of a revised manuscript is final. A rejection notice received after the initial review may contain words of hope such as, "Because the criticisms raised by the reviewer are of a fundamental nature, we regret to inform you that we are unable to accept this paper for publication in the *Journal of Scientific Research*. If it is possible to revise the paper to overcome the reviewer's criticisms, we may reconsider it." Other rejections may offer no hope for reconsideration.

Sometimes, rejections are based on factors other than scientific soundness. Consider this one: "Your paper, which you kindly submitted for publication, has been reviewed by an outside referee and a member of our Editorial Board. They believe that it is likely to be of interest primarily to a narrow range of specialists and it is therefore unsuitable for publication in the *Journal*. I regret that we cannot accept it."

Rejection letters are received by the best of scientists. Appropriate responses to rejection notices are to evaluate the scientific basis for criticisms, revise the work accordingly, and seek another journal or publisher. Veteran writers will confess to receiving numerous rejection notices, but for many of the manuscripts that were initially reviewed unfavorably, ultimate publication resulted in rave reviews or scores of reprint requests. Occasionally, reviews reveal fatal flaws in a work that make it unsuitable for publication. The above situations characterize the publishing world, and it is important for researchers to develop the tenacity necessary to survive in it.

Handling Proofs

Manuscripts that are typeset go through a proofing stage. The process involves review and revision of typeset material on legal-sized sheets known as galley proofs. It is the author's responsibility to peruse galley proofs for errors introduced during typesetting and to make changes using proofreaders' marks (Table 10-1), the uses of which are exemplified in Figure 10-1. Galley proofs may also contain questions from editors. These author queries should be answered succinctly in the margins.

Proofs of papers may be received shortly before the print date; thus, proofreading should be completed within 48 hours. Avoid mak-

Table 10-1. Proofreaders' Marks and Margin Instructions for Printers

Instruction	Mark in text	Mark in Margin
Capitalize	dragendorff reagent	*cap*
Close up	mouse Ig G	⌒
Delete	have in in vitro	*le*
Insert comma	In mammals pentoxifylline	⋏
Insert hyphen	high performance	=
Insert period	during screening However,	⊙
Insert semicolon	respectively meter calibrated	⋏;
Insert space	nuclei acids	#
Insert word	trace molecular weight	# *low* #
Make lowercase	Keto-reductase activity	*l.c.*
Start new paragraph	by rDNA methods. The next	¶
Subscript	-CH₂-CH₃	⌄2 ⌄3
Superscript	14C	⌄14
Transpose	metabolite	*tr*
Set in roman type	Most *fungi* are	*rom*
Set in italic type	trans-Stilbene	*ital*
Set in boldface type	Instrumentation	*b.f.*
Let it stand	make the calibration	*stet*

ing revisions in the copy unless they are absolutely necessary. Author-initiated changes at the galley-proof stage can delay publication and may result in a charge for services.

The corrected proofs should be returned by first-class mail to the printer. Be careful to note the printer's address. It is frequently different from that of the editor or publisher.

The proofing of book-length manuscripts cannot be completed in 48 hours. The printer, however, is likely to have a deadline and may ask that you expedite the proofing step. One or two weeks is a typical allotment for this task.

Figure 10-1. Examples of the use of proofreaders' marks and margin instructions.

I have composed this paragraph	*tr*
to show you how proofreaders'	*ℐ*
marks are used on galley or	*#*
page proofs. You should note	⊙
special instructions that may	*l.c.*
be given by the publisher on	*#*
the use of english, technical	*cap*
expressions, etc. Also,	*ital*
the proofs may contain	
questions that should be	
answered succinctly in	*ℓe*
the margins. Try to	*stet ⁋*
return the corrected proofs	
within 48 hours to the	*of receipt*
printer. Be sure to	
note the correct address	
of the printer although it	⋏
may be the same as the	
publisher.	

Requests for purchase orders for reprints and page charges will often accompany galley proofs. An advisor will have to approve these purchases from a university account, and it will take some prognosticating to anticipate reprint needs. Until publication, an accepted paper may be referred to as "in press" or "accepted for publication" in interim papers and reports. Before acceptance, papers are referred to as "unpublished results" (in footnotes or parentheses) and are usually excluded from bibliographies.

Acceptance and publication of the first paper are important milestones in a scientist's career. Seeing one's name in print provides the thrill experienced by performers who see their "name in lights." The experience with reprints of a researcher's first paper has been aptly described by Slobodkin: "Reprints of his first published paper are sent to parents and grandparents; and the first reprint requests from strangers in Iowa or, better still, agricultural stations in India and Brazil produce a tremendous elation."[5]

Presentation and publication are terminating points in research projects. Many of these projects, however, require attention to special populations (e.g., animals, human subjects) or unusual handling procedures (e.g., biohazards). These topics are covered in the next chapter.

References

[1] R. A. Day, *How to Write and Publish a Scientific Paper*, 4th ed. (Phoenix: Oryx Press, 1994).

[2] E. J. Bauer, The "KISS" method for speaker slide preparation: Keep it simple, stupid! *Medical Meetings* 4 (3) (1977), p. 32.

[3] A. J. MacGregor, Preparing poster talks, IEEE (Institute of Electrical and Electronics Engineers) *Transactions on Professional Communications* PC-12 (1978), pp. 103–5.

[4] AAUP *Directory* (New York: The Association of American University Presses, 1994/95).

[5] L. B. Slobodkin, Scientific sterility in middle age, *American Scientist* 59 (1971), pp. 678–79.

RESEARCH WITH HUMAN SUBJECTS, ANIMALS, AND BIOHAZARDS

> *The history of liberty has largely been the observance of procedural safeguards.*
>
> —Felix Frankfurter

Scientists operate under three suppositions: (1) research is beneficial to society, (2) researchers are benevolent and trustworthy, and (3) scientific research is nonpolitical. The ethical correlates to these tenets are (1) research is justified based on favorable risk/benefit ratios, (2) researchers should be responsible for the conduct of research, and (3) researchers should be self-governing and self-regulating.

Unfortunately, history attests to exceptions to these ideals, which have led to the passage of laws and adoption of regulations, particularly in research with human subjects, animals, and biohazards. The regulations are promulgated by governmental bodies and are about as interesting to read as telephone directories. Nevertheless, scientists must know and abide by the regulations. Otherwise, more restrictive legislation is likely in the future. Historical perspectives and interpretive reviews are offered here to help researchers comply with federal, state, and local regulations on research involving human subjects, animals, and biosafety (i.e., recombinant DNA, infectious organisms, radioactive materials, toxic chemicals, and dangerous drugs).

Human Subjects Research

Research with human subjects plays an indispensable role in biomedical and social-behavioral sciences. In human subjects research, however, there is a crucial interplay between benefits derived and the risks to subjects.

Historical Background

As noted by Brady and Jonsen, human experimentation predates the first century A.D. when Egyptian physicians "engaged" convicted criminals in vivisection experiments.[1] Many centuries passed before English and German literary movements in the eighteenth and nineteenth centuries produced works that served as a portent of concern for human subjects in research. For example, Mary Shelley's classic 1818 tale of human subjects research, *Frankenstein*, warns scientists about placing research above human feeling.

The nineteenth century witnessed the development of scientific rationalism and the industrial revolution. This was accompanied by a rise in Western individualism, which has been characterized by Joseph Brady (U.S. Food and Drug Administration Workshop Talk, New Orleans, 1978) as an "autonomous challenge to paternalistic practices which were previously assumed to be beneficial to the individual." Simultaneously, there was a shift away from the concept of the physician as strictly a provider of primary care. A sense emerged that the physician had the responsibility to develop knowledge for the benefit of others.

The three research suppositions noted earlier seemed to function for human subjects research through the 1940s. After World War II, however, descriptions of Nazi experiments with human beings shocked and horrified humanity. The world could no longer rely on the a priori benevolence of researchers.

To provide a basis for conviction of the Nazi criminals during the Nuremberg Trials, the United States Military Tribunal developed a set of guidelines for conducting human experimentation. Briefly, these rules stated that (1) voluntary consent by subjects is essential, (2) subjects cannot be used except when research results can be obtained in no other way and when prior animal studies indicate that disability and death will not occur, (3) the expected benefits must outweigh the risks, (4) only qualified investigators will conduct research, (5) subjects can withdraw at will, and (6) research is terminated if risks increase during experimentation.

After the Nuremberg Trials, the World Medical Association and medical societies in the United States and the United Kingdom adopted ethical codes worded similarly to the above recommendations. Despite these commitments and the requirement of consent forms mandated by the 1962 amendments to the 1938 Food, Drug, and Cosmetic Act, serious violations of human rights continued in biomedical experimentation through the early 1960s.

In 1966, a Harvard medical researcher, Henry Beecher, documented 22 examples of studies, published in reputable medical journals, that revealed serious breaches in ethics.[2] Included in the Beecher article were the infamous Willowbrook Study and what became known as the (New York) Jewish Chronic Disease Hospital Case. In the Willowbrook Study, infectious hepatitis was induced in mentally defective children. While the parents gave consent to injection or oral administration of the virus, they were not informed of the hazards involved. In the Jewish Chronic Disease Hospital case, live cancer cells were injected into 22 human subjects as part of a study of immunity to the disease. The subjects were just told that they "would be receiving some cells"; the word "cancer" was not used.

In the 1960s, experiments in social psychology, which involved deceit, came under attack by social-behavioral scientists, ethicists, and governmental administrators. As noted by Hunt, the indignation was principally against work published in 1963 by Stanley Milgram at Yale.[3] Milgram sat naive subjects before a bogus control panel and instructed them to administer progressively more powerful "electric shocks" to Milgram's unseen confederates, who were linked to the "control room" by intercom. The subjects were unaware of the confederacy or the fact that no electrical shocks were being administered. Milgram instructed the subjects to continue the administration of "shocks" even after mock grunts, cries, and screams were heard over the intercom. He reported subsequently that a number of the subjects "were observed to sweat, tremble, stutter, bite their lips, groan, and dig their fingernails into their flesh"; yet, most of them obeyed Milgram's orders. Milgram justified his work by stating he was developing an understanding of normal human behavior. Ironically, this type of reasoning contributed to the excesses in Nazi Germany during the 1930s and 1940s.

Milgram's experiments, the Beecher article, and, finally, revelations in the early 1970s of the Tuskegee Study, all influenced federal legislative action.

The Tuskegee case originated in the 1930s when the U.S. Public Health Service began studying the long-term effects of syphilis in men. Two groups of African American men were chosen for the investigation, which was conducted at a penal institution in Tuskegee, Alabama. One group had syphilis; the second was disease free. Through the next 30 years, the men were given normal health care but no treatment for syphilis. Thus, the study extended well into the time when antibiotics were available for the effective treatment of syphilis.

Americans were shocked by the Tuskegee Study. Congress reacted by passing the National Research Act, which was signed into law on July 12, 1974. This act provided for interim regulations for the conduct of biomedical and social-behavioral research. Simultaneously, the National Commission for the Protection of Human Subjects of Biomedical and Behavioral Research was established. The Commission's 1979 report, popularly referred to as the Belmont Report[4] (after an intensive series of discussions held in the Smithsonian Institution's Belmont Conference Center), was well received and became the basis for amended regulations[5] that are now in force.

Current Regulations

The federal regulations for human subjects research[5] are applicable only to federally sponsored research. Under the "principle of preemption," states, municipalities, and other bodies may not pass laws that lessen the impact of federal statutes. Lower legislative bodies, and universities through institutional policy, may, however, augment federal laws with their own rules and regulations. Indeed, many universities apply federal regulations uniformly to research, regardless of sources of funding. Thus, researchers must find out about applicable regulations for human subjects research at their institutions. Fortunately, the composite rules are contained in a university's Institutional General Assurance (IGA). IGAs are approved by the Department of Health and Human Services (DHHS, National Institutes of Health, Office for Protection from Research Risks [OPRR], Bethesda, MD) as a basis for regulating human subjects research at institutions that accept federal funds. This includes practically all institutions of higher learning in the United States.

It is important to obtain a copy of a university's IGA (or equivalent policy document) through the university's sponsored-research office. After one has read it, questions should be directed to the staff of the sponsored-research office or to the chairperson of a university's Institutional Review Board (IRB) (see below).

The IGA commits an institution to policy and procedures to ensure that subjects do not engage in research without being properly informed. Informed consent involves the following characteristics:

1. *Information.* Subjects are given information on procedures, possible benefits, risks, and qualifications of investigators before making judgments about participation.
2. *Understanding.* Investigators take measures to ensure that subjects understand the consequences of participation in the research.

3. *Voluntariness*. Subjects are given opportunities to contemplate their decision to participate, and they give consent without coercion and with the understanding that they may withdraw at any time.

The informed consent procedure must be carefully designed and administered. Its completion is documented by a consent form. The consent form, therefore, is principally a legal instrument designed to protect the investigator and the institution. Guidelines for the preparation of consent forms are given in the Appendix.

Some social science researchers employ deception. That is, to assure experimental validity, the subjects cannot be informed of all the elements of the research. Investigators argue that without this deception they cannot accurately assess human behavior since subjects might modify their actions according to what they think is expected. An extreme example of deception is the Milgram "shock" experiment described earlier. While experiments like this are unlikely to be approved under current regulations, research involving deception can be approved under the following conditions:

1. Deception is necessary and alternative procedures are not available.
2. The deceptive procedure will not place subjects at significant physical, psychological, social, or financial risk.
3. The experiments are followed by careful debriefing sessions during which the subjects are fully informed.

Certain types of research are considered innocuous enough to permit an exempted or IRB-sanctioned expedited review (see below).[5] These categories of research include:

1. Research conducted in established or commonly accepted educational settings, and research that involves normal educational practices.
2. Research involving the use of educational tests (cognitive, diagnostic, aptitude, achievement) if information taken from these sources is recorded so that subjects cannot be identified.
3. Research involving survey or interview procedures, except where all of the following conditions exist:
   a. responses are recorded so that human subjects can be identified, directly or through identifiers linked to the subjects;
   b. the subject's responses, if they become known outside the research, could place the subject at risk of criminal or civil liability or be damaging to the subject's financial standing;

    c. the research deals with sensitive aspects of the subject's own behavior.

4. Research involving the observation (including observation of participants) of public behavior, except where all of the following conditions exist:
    a. observations are recorded so that the human subjects can be identified;
    b. the observations recorded about the individual, if they became known outside the research, could place the subject at risk;
    c. the research deals with sensitive aspects of the subject's own behavior.

5. Research involving the collection or study of existing data, documents, records, pathological specimens, or diagnostic specimens if these sources are publicly available or if the information is recorded so that subjects cannot be identified.

The "principle of preemption" applies to the expedited reviews, and it should be determined whether a university's IGA prescribes stricter rules. Whether exempted, expedited, or regular IRB-reviewed (see below) research is conducted, it is wise and ethically appropriate to make sure that subjects are as informed as possible.

Institutional Review Boards

Society recognizes the importance of human subjects research. It also strives to protect the powerless. Subjects enlisted in studies are generally naive about the research process. Their participation may be the first activity of its type in their lives. These individuals deserve the protection of informed consent and peer review. The peer review process is accomplished through an IRB.

An IRB is a committee appointed by the university's president, but oversight of the committee's actions is delegated to the chief research officer of the university (e.g., vice president of research or equivalent). The IRB has the following makeup:[5]

- At least five members of varying backgrounds and expertise
- Neither all men or women, or members entirely from one profession
- At least one member from a nonscientific area (e.g., law, ethics, or theology)
- At least one member who is not affiliated with the institution or is not a member of a family of an employee of the institution

The IRB's chief responsibility is to decide whether research projects place subjects at risk. If so,

- Will the risks be outweighed by the benefits to the subject and the knowledge to be gained from the study?
- Will the rights and welfare of subjects be adequately protected?
- Will ethically appropriate and legally effective informed consent be secured from subjects?

Considerations of research purpose and design are not directly at issue in these judgments. However, if a proposal is scientifically flawed so that no valid conclusions can be reached, the IRB should reject the proposal based on a poor risk/benefit ratio. The IRB also has the authority to institute monitoring systems to ensure the rights and welfare of subjects.

IRBs meet according to guidelines set forth in IGAs. Typically, meetings are held once or twice a month. Prior to their meetings, the IRB members receive copies of investigators' proposals. Sponsored-projects office staff know when the IRB meets and what type of documentation is necessary for the review purpose. Usually, a proposal synopsis will have to be prepared by the investigator. The synopsis accompanies the protocol and contains information such as:

1. Requirements for the subject population, and, if applicable, the rationale for using special groups such as prisoners, children, the mentally infirm, or groups whose abilities to give voluntary consent may be impaired.
2. Potential risks (physical, psychological, social, or legal), their seriousness, and the likelihood of their occurrence. If there are potential risks, other methods that were considered should be described and indications given why these methods will not be used.
3. The consent procedures to be followed, including how and when informed consent will be obtained and an explanation if consent will not be obtained.
4. Procedures, including confidentiality safeguards, for protecting against and minimizing risks, and a description of their likely effectiveness.
5. The potential benefits to be gained by subjects, and benefits that may accrue to society as a result of the planned investigation.
6. The risk/benefit ratio and an explanation of how it was computed.

Note that the proposal synopsis contains references to many of the concerns considered under the earlier discussions on informed consent and the preparation of a consent form. Thus, preparation of these items should be done at the same time.

Often a proposal can be submitted to a funding agency before it is reviewed by the IRB. This assumes, of course, that the review will occur prior to a decision on funding. For example, the National Institutes of Health (NIH) permits submission of nonreviewed proposals. The IRB, however, must approve or reconcile any points of contention between the investigator and the committee within 60 days of submission. If irreconcilable differences exist or the proposal is disapproved, it must be withdrawn from the NIH. Some universities require that the review process be completed before a proposal leaves campus. It is important to ascertain the procedure used at your institution.

Some universities have a two-tiered review system. This means that proposals are normally reviewed at the departmental level before being considered by the IRB. Alternatively, certain low-risk studies may call for review and approval by only one or two members of the IRB (so-called expedited review).[5] One additional option occurs with proposals for other low-risk ("exempt") research that may only require review at the departmental level. The IGA, sponsored-projects officer, or the chairpersons of the departmental committee and the IRB chairperson are good sources of information on procedures and regulations.

A typical procedure for preparing human subjects research proposals might be as follows:

1. Develop the research hypothesis.
2. Design the study and prepare the proposal, taking into consideration:
   a. the procedures for informed consent
   b. the consent form
   c. the synopsis of the proposal.
3. Obtain counsel through your advisor and the departmental review committee or its equivalent (e.g., departmental research committee).
4. Submit the proposal to IRB for review.

If an IRB or departmental review committee requests changes in the human subjects aspects of a proposal, the requests should be clarified before proceeding. Also, the action necessary to document the changes should be determined. Researchers should not be afraid to seek information and advice from committee chairpersons or members. In the process, determine whether it is customary for investigators to attend department or IRB meetings convened to review a protocol. A visit with an IRB chairperson is also helpful when communications between an investigator and the committee have been difficult. The IRB chairperson and IRB members are researchers, and they understand the struggles necessary to comply with regulations.

Good investigators empathize with their subjects and appreciate the need for regulations. This is best understood by being a subject in research yourself—a role that should be played by all human subjects researchers at some time.

A researcher experiences a sense of satisfaction when she or he has had a protocol approved by an IRB. Once that happens, however, the major responsibility for the rights and welfare of subjects falls on the researcher's shoulders. Researchers must see that protocols are followed properly. If problems arise, it is the researcher's responsibility to inform the IRB promptly. Few research activities involve greater responsibilities and professional acumen than those involving human subjects.

Use of Animals in Research

The importance of animals in research can be traced to the late eighteenth century, when scientists began to use animals for models to study human diseases. For example, Edward Jenner in 1798 used a cowpox preparation to inoculate humans against smallpox after discovering a low incidence of smallpox in milkmaids. Robert Koch and Louis Pasteur used animals during the latter part of the 1800s to elucidate the correlation between "germ" exposure and diseases. The famous canine experiments of Banting and Best in the 1920s uncovered a cause for diabetes mellitus in mammals. The latter work was a portent of the extensive animal experimentation and biomedical advances in North America that have occurred during the past several decades. These include:[6]

- Primate models for the study of Alzheimer's disease and AIDS;
- Development of cancer chemotherapy and the first demonstrated link between cancer and infectious agents through experiments in dogs;
- Development of toxicological screening methods using mice and rats;
- Development of therapies for and prevention of beriberi, rubella, pertussis, pellagra, measles, mumps, and diphtheria through experiments with mice, rats, chickens, and dogs.

The list extends to every area of biomedical research.[6] The results of decades of research have benefited hundreds of millions of people worldwide.

Besides the above-noted positive benefits to human medicine, animal research has been essential in advancing animal health care, including the following:[6]

- Vaccine development (e.g., distemper, rabies, and tetanus);
- Surgical treatment of hip dysplasia in dogs;
- Successful treatment of feline leukemia;
- Pet nutrition.

Animal research in the agricultural sciences in the United States can be traced to the Hatch Act, which was passed by Congress in 1887 to "aid in acquiring and diffusing among the people of the United States useful and practical information on subjects connected with agriculture, and to promote scientific investigation and experiment respecting the principles and applications of agricultural science." Together, agricultural and veterinary medical researchers have decreased the incidence and severity of animal diseases, bettered the nutritional status of farm animals, and improved the quality of life of both wild and domestic animals.

The use of animals in behavioral research began in the late nineteenth and early twentieth centuries when investigators at Clark University in Worcester, Massachusetts, studied the behavior of rats placed in mazes, in problem boxes, and on revolving drums. Animal behavioral psychology received its first serious recognition as a subdiscipline in 1915, when John B. Watson was elected president of the American Psychological Association. Watson's influential book, *Behavior: An Introduction to Comparative Psychology*, was published a year earlier and served as a basis for the extensive animal-based psychological research that has been conducted to the present.

Humane Treatment of Animals

Our interest in animals has ancient roots. Humans began caring for animals that were picked up in the wild. Early domestication attempts, perhaps as long as 10,000 years ago, were probably for practical reasons such as the use of wolves and wild dogs in hunting societies. While displaying fondness for animals, humans have also historically displayed a potential for animal cruelty. During the Renaissance, social activists, particularly in England, began to speak out against cruelty to animals.

Antivivisectionist movements in nineteenth-century England captured the sympathy of Queen Victoria, who formed a Royal Commission and charged it with the study of animal cruelty during experimentation. The recommendations of the Commission led to the Cruelty to Animals Act of 1876. This nineteenth-century act served as legal precedent for current U.S. laws governing the care and treatment of animals in research.

Unfortunately, the intent of antivivisectionist and many animal rights groups throughout the twentieth century has been the ban of all animal experimentation. These groups suggest that we receive little benefit from animal research and assert that it could be replaced totally by *in vitro* and computer methods. People espousing such positions are ill informed.

The benefits of animal research to human and animal medicine are irrefutable[6,7] but have accrued with some risks and discomfort to animals. While advances have been made through *in vitro* and computer modeling, a 1986 study by the Office of Technology Assessment of the U.S. Congress notes: "The outright replacement of animals with non-animal methods in research is not at hand, and, because of the nature of biomedical and behavioral research, in many instances it is not likely to become feasible."[8] This assessment will probably hold well into the future. Accordingly, animal research will not be abolished.

There is, however, a heightened sensitivity in the scientific world to animals' welfare in research, due in part to research conducted by comparative psychologists and ethologists during the past century.[9] Collectively, scientists have come to recognize a behavioral corollary to Darwinian evolution—a continuum of emotional awareness, consciousness, and intelligence across different animal species.[9,10] Thus, regulations and procedures have been developed to help ensure the welfare of animals—animals that must be used to advance knowledge, to aid research of direct benefit to animals, and to support research that will provide improved methods, devices, and drugs for the prevention and treatment of diseases in nonhuman and human animals.

Animal Welfare Legislation and Regulations

After World War II, biomedical research increased markedly in the United States, however, not without some abuses by researchers and animal suppliers. Activities by animal rights groups and a heightened awareness of animal welfare issues by the public elicited responses from the federal government. A series of surveys of animal research performed by the NIH in the 1960s led to the passage of the Animal Welfare Act of 1966 (and amendments in 1970, 1976, and 1985) and publication of the *Guide for the Care and Use of Laboratory Animals*, which was updated in 1996.[11] The *Guide*, plus regulations of the Animal and Plant Health Inspection Service (APHIS) of the United States Department of Agriculture (USDA),[12] contains minimum requirements for the handling, maintenance, and transportation of live vertebrate animals.

Institutions receiving NIH funds for research with animals must submit an assurance document to the OPRR (i.e., the same agency that regulates human subjects research) committing these institutions to the principles in the *Guide*. The same institutions must also agree to a minimum of twice-yearly inspections of facilities by APHIS professionals. All researchers who use animals in research should have a copy of the *Guide*, which is available through the www.[11]

A university's animal research IGA requires establishment of an Institutional Animal Care and Use Committee (IACUC, pronounced "I-a-cook") to approve and review animal research activities on campus. The IACUC is appointed by the university's president, but oversight of the committee's actions is delegated to the chief research officer of the university (e.g., vice president of research or equivalent). An IACUC must have at least five members whose background and experience is relevant to the committee's responsibilities. At least one member of the committee must be a veterinarian who is likely to be responsible for animal care at the institution (i.e., campus veterinarian). The committee must also have at least one non-scientist member and a member who is unaffiliated with the institution. Like human subjects research regulations, animal research guidelines can be strengthened by state or local statutes and by university policies. The chairperson of the IACUC or the campus veterinarian can supply a copy of an institution's guidelines.

The guiding principles of animal research are as follows:

Personnel

1. Experiments with live vertebrate animals and tissues from living animals must be conducted under the supervision of qualified biological, behavioral, and medical scientists.
2. Housing, care, and feeding of experimental animals must be supervised by a qualified veterinarian.

Research

1. Research must be designed to yield results for the good of society. Experiments must not be random or unnecessary.

2. Experiments should be based on knowledge of diseases or problems under study with anticipated results that justify their performance.

3. Mathematical models and *in vitro* biological systems should be used when possible to reduce the numbers of animals needed.

4. All unnecessary suffering and injury to animals must be avoided during experimentation.

5. Investigators must terminate experiments when it is believed that continuation may result in unnecessary suffering and injury to animals.

6. If experiments are likely to cause greater discomfort than that attending anesthetization, animals must be treated appropriately with an analgesic. Cases in which drug treatment defeats the purpose of the experiment and data cannot be obtained by any other humane procedure are the only exceptions to this rule. Such experiments must be scrupulously supervised by qualified senior scientists.

7. Postexperimental care of animals must minimize discomfort and consequences of any disability resulting from the experiment, in accordance with acceptable veterinary practice.

8. Euthanasia must be accomplished in a humane manner using acceptable practices and ensuring immediate death.[13] No animal should be disposed of until death is certain.

Facilities and Transportation

1. Standards for construction and use of housing, service, and surgical facilities should meet those described in the *Guide*.[11]

2. Transportation of animals must meet standards and regulations intended to reduce discomfort, stress, and spread of disease.[12] All animals received for experimental purposes must be promptly uncrated and placed in permanent facilities.

Veterinary Care and Assistance

Laboratory animal medicine (LAM) has emerged during at least the past forty years as a specialty of veterinary medicine. LAM professionals are typically graduate veterinarians who have advanced research degrees or postdoctoral training. The *Guide*[11] and attendant legislation of the Animal Welfare Act require that universities receiving NIH support provide "adequate veterinary care" for animals used in research. This care is generally supplied by a LAM specialist who may also head a centralized animal research facility. Researchers who conduct animal experiments should know the LAM specialists on their campuses.

The LAM specialist contributes to the following stages of animal research:

1. Procurement of animals
2. Receipt, quarantine, evaluation, and approval of animals for experimentation
3. Consultation and collaboration during research

Universities generally use central procurement procedures for animals. The procurement procedures will typically require paperwork that includes information on species, strain, and number of animals needed, as well as descriptions of their proposed use (i.e., IACUC-approved protocol that indicates allowable numbers of animals) in research. Special instructions for handling may also be requested. The LAM specialist can advise researchers on the proper selection of species or strains, the statistical validity of the numbers of animals proposed for a study, and cost factors.

Once animals are received, they are quarantined. The quarantine period helps animals adjust to new environments and recover from shipping stress. LAM professionals also observe the animals during the quarantine period and perform diagnostic tests. Necessary treatment or vaccinations can be given to prevent introduction of diseases into established colonies. Lang indicated that quarantine periods vary with species but are as follows for common laboratory animals: mouse and rat, 5 days; guinea pig and hamster, 7 days; cat, dog, and rabbit, 14 days; nonhuman primates, 30 days.[14] The lengths of quarantine periods should be considered when estimating the time needed from day of ordering to day of experimentation. Also, an advisor's approval will be necessary before ordering animals. Besides procurement charges, most universities assess per diem charges for animals to cover feeding, watering, and cage-cleaning costs.

The LAM specialist should be consulted on health and general welfare concerns that arise during experimentation. If animals die unexpectedly during an experiment, it is important that the veterinarian determine whether the cause of death is related to the experimental treatment and take measures to prevent the spread of infectious diseases when necessary. The LAM specialist can also be considered as a possible collaborator in research projects. The expertise of a veterinary scientist can add considerable strength in many areas of research. This is particularly true in projects requiring surgery, histopathology, chronic treatments, and animal modeling. LAM specialists can also make unique contributions during service on dissertation committees.

Biohazards

Potential or real biohazards include recombinant DNA molecules, etiologic agents (e.g., viral, bacterial, fungal, parasitic agents), oncogenic viruses, and chemicals that are radioactive or potentially toxic (including carcinogenicity) to animals and humans. A variety of federal guidelines or standards exist for the handling and disposal of these agents.

Recombinant DNA *Molecules*

The first significant research efforts with recombinant DNA material occurred in the early 1970s. As noted by Fredrickson, the first few years of recombinant DNA research were marked by controversy.[15] The potential hazards of inserting foreign genetic material into common gut bacteria such as *Escherichia coli* were either overstated or misunderstood. Cautious progress in this field of research has given scientists and federal officials more realistic perspectives that have been used to prepare the most recently adopted guidelines.[16] These guidelines have less force of law than the regulations governing human and animal research; however, researchers will find that most universities have adopted them.

The guidelines recommend the formation of an Institutional Biosafety Committee (IBC), which reviews and approves the construction and handling of recombinant DNA molecules and microorganisms (including viruses) containing recombinant DNA molecules. In the context of the guidelines, recombinant DNA molecules are (1) molecules constructed outside living cells by joining natural or synthetic DNA segments to DNA molecules, which are subsequently replicated in a living cell, or (2) DNA molecules replicated as a result of the steps in (1). If a synthetic DNA segment is not expressed *in vivo*, yielding a biologically active polynucleotide or polypeptide, then it is exempt from the guidelines.

Like the IRB and IACUC, the IBC is appointed by the university's president, but oversight of the committee's actions is delegated to the chief research officer of the university (e.g., vice president of research or equivalent). The IBC consists of no fewer than five members who have collective expertise in recombinant DNA technology. They must also be capable of assessing the safety of recombinant DNA research and the risks of this research to public health and the environment. At least two members of the IBC must be unaffiliated with the university and should represent public health and environmental interests of the surrounding community. The IBC on many campuses will be responsible for all biohazards (see below), not just those associated with recombinant DNA molecules.

The IBC's responsibility in recombinant DNA research is to evaluate proposals for potential hazards and to ensure that suitable precautions are adopted. Investigations are divided into four categories:

1. Experiments requiring review and approval by the DHHS Recombinant DNA Advisory Committee (RAC), the NIH, and the IBC. Certain experiments (e.g., release of an agriculturally important recombinant microorganism) may require approval by other agencies (e.g., the USDA and the Environmental Protection Agency [EPA]).
2. Experiments needing IBC review and approval only.
3. Experiments that require only notification of the IBC before implementation.
4. Experiments exempt from IBC review.

Increasingly sophisticated physical containment systems are required for the more potentially dangerous laboratory experiments. The physical facilities are categorized as BL1, BL2, BL3, and BL4, with BL4 involving the most stringent containment. The federal guidelines and university policy statements should be consulted for more extensive descriptions of containment conditions and review procedures, respectively. The IBC chairperson is a good source of information and advice. He or she may also provide an institutional policy statement that should be consulted if work is planned with any recombinant DNA or other potential biohazards that are defined as the responsibility of the IBC.

Microbiological Hazards

Etiologic agents and oncogenic viruses are two biohazards that require special handling. Federal regulations have not been promulgated in these areas, although standards have been published by the Centers for Disease Control (CDC) and the NIH.[17] The latter document also contains references to papers as well as recommendations for research with viruses and other etiologic agents implicated in acquired immune deficiency syndrome (AIDS). The use of etiologic agents and oncogenic viruses is often regulated by an IBC, and the committee's chairperson is a good source of additional information on these agents and the policies and procedures relevant to their use in research.

Radiation Hazards, Toxic Chemicals, and Dangerous Drugs

The use of devices emitting ionizing radiation or radioactive materials, toxic chemicals (including carcinogens), and dangerous drugs in research are regulated by university safety officers who have relevant oversight responsibilities. It is important to locate these individuals for appropriate documents on university policies and guidelines.

The radiation safety officer may serve under the auspices of a radiation safety committee (RSC), which is appointed analogously to the IRB, IACUC, and IBC. The radiation safety program is devised in conjunction with the RSC and is maintained on a day-to-day basis by a radiation safety officer who is responsible for:

1. Termination of activities causing radiation hazards.
2. Inspection of areas where sources of radiation are stored or used in research.
3. Enforcement of a program of procurement and record keeping required of all authorized users of radioactive sources or materials.
4. Maintenance of systems for the proper disposal of radioactive wastes.
5. Management of educational programs on safety precautions and procedures.
6. Ensuring that new radiation sources are kept in compliance with federal and state regulations.
7. Service as liaison between university officials and federal and state officials to assure fulfillment of radiation safety and licensure requirements.

To use radioactive sources and materials, researchers will have to obtain approval through the radiation safety officer. Usually, an advisor will be the authorized user who may supervise relevant activities by students. This magnifies the students' responsibilities and requires that they become well informed.

A copy of the university's radiation safety manual should be obtained through the radiation safety office. Enrollment in one or more radiation safety courses may be required before certification for use of regulated sources or radioactive materials is received. Even if one's background is in physics or chemistry, the practical insights gained through radiation safety courses will be valuable.

The university's safety office is responsible for the pickup and proper disposal of toxic chemicals. It is important to find out what waste containers are to be used for temporary containment. The proper routine for requesting permanent disposal should also be determined. Researchers should assiduously avoid disposal of chemicals in sinks or common sewer drains.

Researchers should know about the biological effects of toxic and carcinogenic chemicals. Standard reference works and WWW sources contain useful toxicity data.[18–20] Recommendations for containment and minimization of contact with toxic and carcinogenic chemicals should be in force in relevant laboratories. Briefly, inhalation of toxic chemicals should be minimized through the use of fume hoods, and skin and eye contact should be prevented by appropriate coverings. Safety-office personnel are usually able to check the efficiency of fume hoods.

Various potent drugs are useful tools in biological research. When the required drugs have a high abuse potential, the Drug Enforcement Administration (DEA) of the Department of Justice may have categorized them as Scheduled Drugs under the Controlled Substances Act of 1970. Following are examples of drugs or drug-containing dosage forms listed under Schedules I through V, with drugs of greatest abuse potential in Schedule I.

Schedule I

- Opiates, e.g., acetylmethadol
- Opium derivatives, e.g., heroin
- Hallucinogenic substances, e.g., lysergic acid diethylamide (LSD), marijuana
- Depressants, e.g., methaqualone
- Stimulants, e.g., N,N-dimethylamphetamine

Schedule II

- Certain substances of vegetable origin or chemical synthesis (or salts or chemically equivalent substances), e.g., codeine, raw opium
- Opium poppy and poppy straw
- Coca leaves and any salt, compound, derivative, or preparation of coca leaves, e.g., cocaine, ecgonine

Schedule III

- Less potent stimulants, e.g., chlorphentermine
- Less potent depressants, e.g., pentobarbital
- Anabolic steroids, e.g., norethandrolone

Schedule IV

- Weak depressant drugs, e.g., chloral hydrate, meprobamate
- Weak stimulants, e.g., pemoline

Schedule V

- Miscellaneous drugs of abuse, e.g., mixtures or pharmaceutical preparations containing no more than 200 milligrams of codeine per 100 milliliters

A more complete listing of scheduled drugs is available through the DEA.[21] The use of scheduled substances in laboratory research, including use with research subjects, requires the permission of an authorized user such as an advisor who may be registered by the DEA. Alternatively, internal authorization procedures, especially for nonresearch subject use, may be possible through the university's safety office. Regardless of the authorization procedure, use of scheduled drugs requires strict accounting procedures, security measures, and assurance of nonuse in humans except under conditions strictly defined and enforced through the university's IRB. Researchers should make sure they understand all these procedures before taking on responsibilities.

The conduct of special types of research, such as those involving human subjects, animals, and biohazards, is aided by guidelines in this chapter. These guidelines will also be helpful during the preparation of grant proposals, which is covered in the next chapter.

References

[1] J. V. Brady and A. R. Jonsen, The evolution of regulatory influences on research with human subjects, in *Human Subjects Research*, R. A. Greenwald, M. K. Ryan, and J. E. Mulvihill, eds. (New York: Plenum Press, 1982), pp. 3–18.

[2] H. K. Beecher, Ethics and clinical research, *New England Journal of Medicine* 274 (1966), pp. 1354–60.

[3] M. Hunt, Research through deception, *New York Times Magazine*, September 12, 1982, pp. 66, 139–42.

[4] Belmont Report—Ethical principles and guidelines for the protection of human subjects of research; report of the National Commission for the Protection of Human Subjects of Biomedical and Behavioral Research, *Federal Register* 44(76)(1979), pp. 23192–97.

[5] *Code of Federal Regulations*, Title 45 (Public Welfare), Volume 1, Parts 1–199, *Protection of Human Subjects* (Washington, D.C.: U.S. Government Printing Office, 1996); http://frwebgate.access.gpo.gov/cgi-bin/waisgate.cgi?WAISdocID=4182228729+1+0+0&WAISaction=retrieve

[6] *Use of Animals in Biomedical Research—The Challenge and Response, White Paper* (Chicago: American Medical Association, 1992).

[7] A. N. Rowan, *Of Mice, Models and Men: A Critical Evaluation of Animal Research* (Albany, NY: State University of New York Press, 1984).

[8] U.S. Congress, Office of Technology Assessment, *Alternatives to Animal Use in Research, Testing and Education* (Washington, D.C.: U.S. Government Printing Office, 1986), Publication No. OTA-BA-273.

[9] D. R. Griffin, Animal thinking, *American Scientist* 72 (1984), pp. 456–64.

[10] C. Sagan, *The Dragons of Eden* (New York: Ballantine Books, 1977).

[11] *Guide for the Care and Use of Laboratory Animals* (Washington, D.C.: National Academy Press, 1996); http://www.nap.edu/readingroom/books/labrats/

[12] *Code of Federal Regulations*, Title 9 (Animals and Animal Products), Animal Welfare, Chapter 1, Parts 1–3 (Washington, D.C.: U.S. Government Printing Office, 1989).

[13] Report of the AVMA Panel on euthanasia, *Journal of the American Veterinary Medical Association* 173 (1978), pp. 59–72.

[14] C. M. Lang, Scheduling animal use by researchers, *Laboratory Animal* (September/October 1972), pp. 22–24.

[15] D. S. Fredrickson, A history of the recombinant DNA guidelines in the United States, in *Recombinant DNA and Genetic Experimentation*, J. Morgan and W. J. Whelan, eds. (New York: Pergamon Press, 1979), pp. 151–56.

[16] Federal guidelines for research involving recombinant DNA molecules, *Federal Register*, July 5, 1994 (59FR344496); http://www.nih.gov/od/orda/toc.htm

[17] *Biosafety in Microbiological and Biomedical Laboratories*, 3rd ed., Centers for Disease Control and NIH (Washington, D.C.: U.S. Government Printing Office, 1993).

[18] R. H. Dreisbach, *Handbook of Poisoning*, 12th ed. (East Norwalk, CT: Appleton and Lange, 1987).

[19] A.K. Furr, ed., CRC *Handbook of Laboratory Safety*, 3rd ed. (Boca Raton, FL: CRC Press, 1990).

[20] *Toxicological Profile Query* (Washington, D.C.: Agency for Toxic Substances Registry, NIH, current); http://atsdr/.atsdr.cdc.gov:8080/gsql/toxprof.script

[21] *Code of Federal Regulations*, Title 21 (Food and Drugs), Volume 9, Part 1308, Schedules of Controlled Substances (Washington, D.C.: U.S. Government Printing Office, 1996); http://frwebgate.access.gpo.gov/cgi-bin/waisgate.cgi?WAISdocID=4357227508+13+0+0&WAISaction=retrieve

12

GETTING GRANT SUPPORT

You have to be willing to let people laugh at you occasionally. And to have others tell you that your work is not so important. And you have to be willing—four times out of five—to have your grant application turned down by the federal government. But what you can't do, as so many of my colleagues have done, is say, "The hell with this." Science is too important to give up so easily.

—George C. Nace

Grants provide support for research and scholarly activities. They are vital to academic life. Graduate students may apply for a grant or work on one with an advisor; therefore, it is important to know about different grants and granting agencies.

Historical Background

The word "grant" means gift, such as money, land, or other type of support. Grants are at least as old as recorded history. White noted that an entry in the Egyptian *Book of the Dead* refers to a good man who gave a boat to one who had none.[1] The gift served a practical purpose. This is characteristic of grants. Moreover, the ancient grantor may have benefited occasionally from the grantee's gifts of fresh fish. Consequently, the grantor's own interests were also served through the award. This, too, is characteristic of grants.

Grants may be used to set up endowments for perpetual support of activities. Plato's Academy was maintained for hundreds of years by his endowment. The early church used endowments to support schools, almshouses, orphanages, monasteries, and hospitals. British royalty endowed charter companies such as the East India and Hudson Bay Companies, which helped commercial development in rural America.

The Smithsonian Institution in Washington, D.C., was started in 1835 through a grant from James B. Smithson, an amateur natural historian of English birth. The first recorded congressional grant-making act was passed in 1842 and resulted in a $30,000 award to Samuel B. Morse for testing the feasibility for public use of the electromagnetic telegraph system.[1] Morse worked earlier on the basis for the telegraph, and his investigations serve as a precedent for pilot or preliminary studies that continue to be necessary for effective grantspersonship.

The success of the industrial revolution in the United States during the late 1800s helped develop industrial magnates such as Andrew Carnegie, Henry Ford, and John D. Rockefeller. Their extraordinary accumulations of wealth permitted the establishment of foundations that continue to support research and scholarship in the United States. Support from foundations, however, is a small part of the total research and development budget of American universities.

The federal government was a poor supporter of research and development before World War II. During the war, however, impressive results were achieved (e.g., the development of controlled nuclear fission and penicillin) through major funding commitments. Federal support for the physical sciences waned after the war. However, biomedical research through the National Institutes of Health (NIH) received increased support through the late 1940s and the 1950s.

On October 4, 1957, the Soviet Union launched its first sputnik. Americans were upset by the thought of a Soviet-controlled object orbiting the Earth and crossing the United States several times a day. Their distress was exacerbated by anti-Communist sentiments and suggestions that the Soviet Union had suddenly become technologically superior to the United States. Congress responded by improving appropriations for the National Science Foundation (NSF) and other federal grant-making bodies. President Kennedy pledged that the United States would put an astronaut on the moon by 1970. Great Society programs started by President Johnson in the mid-1960s included the goal of improved social welfare. These commitments resulted in unprecedented increases in federal allocations to academic institutions for research and development. But the resulting support did not keep pace with inflation and expansions of the scientific community during the 1970s. The 1980s witnessed substantial increases in funding for research in the physical sciences, although most of this support was directed toward defense-related research.

Federal support for research has remained strong during the 1990s, although efforts to balance the federal budget have placed constraints on growth. Nevertheless, yearly multibillion-dollar appropriations continue to make the federal government the largest supporter of university-based research and development in the United States.

Types of Grants

Academicians commonly refer to "grants," but a grant is only one of six instruments for supporting university research and development. These instruments are:

1. free gift or grant-in-aid
2. grant
3. cooperative agreement
4. contract
5. fellowship
6. scholarship

Free Gift or Grant-in-Aid

A grant-in-aid is money that can be spent at the investigator's discretion. No reports to sponsors are necessary for the expenditure of these funds, but it is wise for the investigator to respect the purpose for which the money was given. Grant-in-aid funds are obtained through alumni donations or fund-raising activities of university development staff, faculty, and administrators. Investigators who do industrially sponsored research have frequent opportunities to solicit free gift funds.

The loose accountability for grant-in-aid funds should not be misconstrued. Investigator discretion has been noted, but the ownership of grants should be understood. Nearly all grants are given to institutions, not to individuals. The awards are administered through the institution's accounting office, and an investigator must abide by the institution's policies for expenditure of funds. The greatest "freedom" is afforded to the investigator with grant-in-aid. The money can be used for salaries and wages, research equipment and supplies, travel to scientific meetings, and office expenses. Moreover, funds can be shifted at the investigator's discretion from one category to another. Free gift money permits maximum flexibility; consequently, this type of funding is the hardest to obtain.

Grant

A grant is a flexible instrument used to support research and scholarly activities. Ideas for grants generally come from investigators who define the scope of projects. The federal government (especially the

NIH), however, will occasionally publish so-called Requests for Applications (RFAs), which announce priority areas for funding—areas for which grant requests are encouraged.

Granting agencies allow changes in the objectives of grants, but accountability is required both in the expenditure of funds and in the conduct of research. Indeed, granting agencies have become more aware in recent years of the need for stated objectives, and they demand evidence of attempts to meet these objectives during the course of awards. This is particularly true for federally sponsored grants.

Cooperative Agreement

A cooperative agreement is similar to a grant, but it provides for more direction by the funding agency during the course of the research. Cooperative agreements have been widely used by the U.S. Department of Agriculture (USDA) and the Environmental Protection Agency (EPA).

Contract

A research contract is an agreement to perform carefully defined research. Thus, there is less flexibility in contract research compared to grant-sponsored research.

The federal government occasionally funds contracts after receiving unsolicited proposals from investigators. More commonly, federally sponsored contracts are publicized through Request for Proposal (RFP) notices in the *Commerce Business Daily* (CBD), and investigators may write for a copy of the RFP.

Jargon used by federal agencies is often confusing. The RFP process is no exception. The "actual" RFP requested by the investigator is a document that outlines the objectives of the contract, the criteria for selecting the contractor, and the guidelines for constructing a budget. The latter includes the government's estimate of the number of person-years (equivalent to the number of men and women working full-time for one year) required to fulfill the objectives of the contract. Occasionally, RFPs have such specific objectives that they seem to have been written by an investigator already working in the area. This may be a clue that the contract is already activated. Contracts, like grants, are evaluated periodically for competitive renewal, and they will be described in the CBD.

The CBD, which contains notices of proposed government procurement actions, contract awards, sales of government property, and other procurement information, is published daily and is available on-line in a searchable format.[2] Qualified investigators can bid upon most contracts listed in the CBD. But a novice investigator has no way of knowing, except by intuition, whether the RFP is related to a contract already awarded to an experienced investigator. Unfortunately, in the cases of renewal contracts, the likelihood of the novice attaining funds is slim.

Industrial contracts, like their government counterparts, involve focused research and relatively little freedom to deviate from stated objectives. Industrial firms may be more generous than federal agencies and provide companion grant-in-aid funds. The costs of the contract are negotiated like a business deal. A request for grant-in-aid is articulated as "profit." The "profit" may be used to support graduate fellowships and the investigator's personal research.

Grants and contracts are awarded to academic institutions in the name of the investigator. Fellowships and scholarships are often awarded to individuals.

Fellowships and Scholarships

Fellowships provide support for master's, predoctoral, and postdoctoral education and research. Scholarships are primarily awards for undergraduate research and study. Descriptions of federal and private fellowship, scholarship, and grant programs are available through various WWW sites, including those that are likely to be accessible through your university's sponsored-research office. If not, the National Council of University Research Administrators (NCURA) maintains a WWW site containing hyperlinks to sponsored-projects offices at more than 100 universities nationwide.[3] Two well-organized sponsored-projects web sites are found at Colorado State University[4] and Washington State University (WSU).[5] The WSU site has a special set of hyperlinks to sources of student fellowships, scholarships, and summer and travel grants.[6]

In addition to investigating opportunities via specific agencies, you can also conduct keyword searches through one of several funding source databases available in most universities. Two of these search systems include the Sponsored Programs Information Network (SPIN)[7] and the Community of Science Funding Opportunities database.[8]

It is worth a few hours' effort to investigate the opportunities available. The effort may be assisted by professionals in the university's sponsored-research office. Such offices are responsible for reviewing (for consistencies of proposals with university policies and resources) and forwarding grant, contract, and fellowship proposals to extramural agencies. These offices are staffed by professionals who are knowledgeable about extramural funding opportunities and can advise your fellowship efforts. Also, advisors and department chairpersons may know of unique sources of fellowship support.

Writing Grant Proposals and Applying for Grants

Grantspersonship is the art of obtaining grants. It involves four skills: (1) identifying resources, (2) contacting granting agencies, (3) preparing proposals, and (4) applying for grants. These skills are important because an advisor may ask for help in obtaining a grant that may be pursued jointly. Also, department chairpersons often encourage students to apply for fellowships, which is similar to competing for research grants.

Many departments require the preparation of an original grant proposal as a part of doctoral candidacy requirements. The proposal may then be defended during an oral examination. This serves two purposes: it helps prepare one for a dissertation oral, and it provides experience necessary for a career in research. Proposal preparation or its equivalent is necessary in academic as well as industrial jobs. Competing for grants is an important part of a scientist's academic life. The industrial scientist may also be involved in efforts to obtain federal grants and contracts. Furthermore, industrial research requires written plans and justifications that are akin to grant proposals.

Writing proposals and applying for grants requires discipline and insights that will be helpful throughout a professional career. Commitment, thoroughness, and patience are essential components of the process. Tolerance of failure is also required, because many proposals are rejected. Overcoming the trauma of rejection is an important lesson for the professional. I know researchers who have received dozens of grants during their lives. This has often meant confronting many times that many rejections. Researchers have to develop emotional strength to survive. Survival skills grow out of the self-confidence that comes from research accomplishments, and these skills are useful in one's personal life as well as at work.

Many books and articles have been written on grantspersonship. It is impossible to thoroughly review the subject in the space allotted. Critical pointers and insights are given below. For more detailed treatment of grants, I recommend the books by White[1] and Ogden.[9]

Identifying Resources

As noted above, various web sites list sources of grants, contracts, and fellowships, including federal agencies, foundations, commercial organizations, and associations.[2-8] Besides the names and addresses of sponsors, it is important to know the sponsors' purposes and activities, assets (in the case of foundations), numbers and types of grants awarded in recent years, values of low and high grants, fields of application, limitations, and rules for applications. For foundations, listings of members of boards of directors should also be sought (see below).

Contacting Grantors

It is a mistake to prepare a proposal before contacting the granting agency. Federal agencies such as the NIH have project officers who are pleased to discuss potential proposals. These officials will be optimistic and encouraging even if an idea is not top priority for their agency. They will also tell a researcher if an idea is not worth pursuing because of limited funding possibilities.

This is a good place to mention authorized contacts with granting agencies. Generally, universities prohibit application for extramural funding for anyone except faculty-level scientists. Thus, it can be inappropriate for a graduate student to contact a granting agency. Students will be permitted, however, to apply directly for fellowships in many programs. An advisor may also enlist the help of graduate students in the early stages of grant seeking.

Foundations and industrial firms should be contacted first by letter. Before corresponding with a foundation, you might consider visiting with a college or university development officer. These professionals (who are most often affiliated with university foundations) are familiar with foundation officials and can offer suggestions for crafting the initial contacts.

Inquiry letters to foundations should be addressed to persons identified through your funding database search, or to the Executive Director or Executive Secretary when explicit instructions are not given. The letters should address the following questions:

1. What is to be done?
2. Why is it worth doing?
3. What are the specific objectives?
4. Who is to do the work?
5. What facilities will be required and are they available?

6. How long will the project take?
7. About how much will the project cost?
8. Can a full proposal be submitted?

The last question may be coupled with an offer to visit foundation officials. If you know a member of the board of trustees, he or she may help you get an appointment. Contacts such as these will not compensate for a poor idea or a shoddy proposal. If a proposal is competitive, however, the influence of a board member is invaluable.

Dermer suggests that an atmosphere of friendliness be created during interviews with foundation officials.[10] Officials will be impressed if a researcher is sincere and can explain the proposed research well. The possibility that the foundation may fund work as proposed can be explored, but a decision on funding should not be expected. Before the end of the interview, one can ask if a written proposal can be submitted. If so, the official should be given an estimate of when the proposal will be received.

There are no foolproof methods for approaching industrial firms for grant support. A variety of strategies have been suggested that may be useful. The most "primitive" situation occurs when a researcher has a good idea for a project but knows of no one in the industry who may provide guidance to a potential source of funds. This requires developing unsolicited written inquiries that should contain the following:

1. A brief description of the research to be done. This should address some problem that currently exists (e.g., extend claims of a presently marketed product or provide a new source or route to a valuable process).
2. An explanation of who will do the work and why they are unusually qualified to perform the needed research. (A curriculum vitae should be included in the mailing.)
3. An estimate of how much time will be required for the project and how much it will cost.
4. A list of facilities and equipment needed to perform the study and whether these are available.
5. A best assessment of the profit potential of the study.
6. An inquiry into the possibility of submitting a full proposal.

The choice of potential sources of support should be based on the apparent interests (product lines) of firms. An inquiry should be directed to a scientist, or a manager or administrator, who is in charge of an appropriate division of the company. Names of logical individuals may be obtained from senior authors of related papers or through one or two judiciously placed phone calls. The industrial firm may request a full proposal. A lack of interest at this stage or following evaluation of the proposal is usually final, and additional follow-ups are futile.

Seeking grant and contract support is like a business venture. There is no substitute for personal contact with individuals who may expedite requests. Personal interactions at scientific or professional meetings, or with former associates who may be employed in a given firm, are invaluable. Preliminary contacts can be capped by an offer to present a seminar at a company that may have an interest in one's field of study.

Preparing Proposals

Grant proposals are prepared according to guidelines similar to the ones recommended in Chapters 8 and 10 for reports and papers. Some granting agencies have their own formats, which should be adopted. If no format is prescribed (e.g., many foundations and industrial firms), the one below is recommended.

1. cover page
2. abstract (with key words underlined)
3. budget
4. biographical sketches of investigators
5. research plan
   a. specific aims
   b. significance and background
   c. pilot studies
   d. methods
   e. collaborative assurance
   f. facilities available
   g. appendices

The cover page and abstract are developed as indicated for reports (Chapter 8), with two additions. Lines should be included on the cover page for the signatures of the principal investigator and the official who will sign for the university. In the abstract, key words can be underlined for emphasis. The underlining should be limited to 10 words.

The budget includes sums for one or more of the following:

1. salaries and wages plus benefits
2. supplies
3. equipment

4. special costs
   a. maintenance of animals
   b. patient fees
   c. rental fees
   d. computer and chemical analyses
5. travel
6. indirect costs
7. subcontracts

Salaries and wages are set by the university's personnel office. A personnel pay schedule should be available to help plan costs of required positions. Supplies include expendable items such as paper, computer supplies, glassware, and chemicals. Requests for equipment costing more than $1,000 must be carefully justified because most agencies are reluctant to support capital expenditures.

Special costs for animal maintenance, patient fees (e.g., payments to patients for participation in research, or professional fees to health professionals for physical examinations before and after research studies), and equipment rental or analysis fees vary from university to university. Telephone calls to appropriate centers on campus should yield fee schedules.

Advice on crafting grant, contract, and fellowship budgets up to this point should also be available from professionals in your university's sponsored-projects office.

Funding agencies are fussy about paying for travel. Consequently, requests for travel funds should be conservative and justified. The total to this point is called "direct cost."

Indirect cost is the surcharge a university assesses to meet basic operating expenses associated with research (e.g., heating, lighting, accounting). It is generally calculated as a percentage of total direct cost or modified total direct cost (i.e., total direct cost minus costs of capital equipment and subcontracts). Subcontracts are developed to fund segments of the research project that can best be done off campus. Rules for implementing subcontracts should be available through a university's sponsored-projects office, including possible indirect-costs rates for these elements of a budget.

Biographical sketches of all investigators should be included in the grant proposal. Each sketch should be no more than two or three pages and should include a list of publications (with titles) that are relevant to the proposed research. The biographical materials should clearly indicate the relationship of each person to the project.

The research plan should be carefully developed using the writing guidelines noted in Chapter 8. A "talking style" is particularly effective in grant proposals. In the methods section, for example, sentences such as "If this experiment fails to give expected results, we will . . ." give the reviewer an impression of investigator maturity—a blend of optimism and realism.

The aims of the proposal should be clear, focused, and attainable in the project period. Most importantly, they must contain good ideas and hypotheses that embrace problems at the forefront of a field of study.

The section on significance and background should include a succinct review of the literature and clear statements about the importance of the work proposed. The background need not include an exhaustive review of the literature. A focused review containing the most important citations is preferable.

The description of pilot studies that led to the proposal can be the most important section of the research plan. Preliminary results support the feasibility of the project and suggest that the total project will not fail. The write-up of pilot work should indicate one's ability to analyze and interpret data and to test hypotheses. If the pilot results have been good, the chances for funding are improved.

The methods section should contain descriptions of the procedures and tests that will be used in the proposed work. Special handling procedures for animals, and safeguards and informed consent procedures for human subjects, should be included. The details should be substantive, but it is not necessary to describe minutiae such as common laboratory operations (e.g., pipetting, solution preparation). It is important to indicate the kinds of data expected (e.g., rates of growth, percent inhibition) and how the data will be analyzed (e.g., t-test). The types of data and analytical results that will be necessary to prove hypotheses should also be indicated.

Collaborative arrangements should be described. Who will be responsible for different segments of the study? How are the different investigators uniquely qualified for their tasks? How will the investigators' work be coordinated? Who is responsible for the preparation of reports?

The facilities available for the investigation should be described. Do not include equipment or laboratory facilities that are only peripherally useful. If needed equipment is housed in another department, describe plans for joint use. Cooperative agreements for joint equipment use, as well as collaborative research efforts, should be documented by letters of support. The letters should be collected as appendix material along with preprints of manuscripts, reports, and charts.

   Fellowship applications containing research proposals should be developed as indicated above. Additionally, the fellowship proposal may require a description of the plan of study. These details should be organized carefully along with documentation of advisory faculty support.

   After a proposal is written, it can be judged against criteria commonly used by peer reviewers. Table 12-1 contains common failings of grant proposals. The major shortcomings are flawed ideas, confused concepts or hypotheses, poor organization, and inadequacies of investigators. Thoughtfulness, dedication, and careful preparation are essential to overcome these shortcomings. Critical reviews by an advisor and "writing friends" will help refine the work.

Table 12-1. Common Shortcomings of Grant Proposals[a]

Proposal Section	Problem
Budget	Excessive funds requested; capital-equipment request unjustified; funds requested are insufficient to complete described project
Biographical sketch and backgrounds of investigators	Investigator inexperienced; insufficient number of investigators
Research plan	Poorly organized; too long; too narrow; improperly focused; poorly written; sloppy preparation; inadequate detail
Aims	Project scientifically premature—requires more pilot work; validity questioned; vague or scientifically unsound; too ambitious; hypotheses poor
Significance and background	Problem of little significance or repeats previous work; assumptions questionable; rationale poor; literature background poor or inadequate
Pilot studies	Pilot work ill conceived; data inappropriately analyzed; experiments lack imagination

Continued on next page

Methods	Methods unsuited to stated objectives; unethical or hazardous procedure proposed; controls poorly conceived or inadequately described; some problems not realized or dealt with properly; results will be confusing, difficult to interpret, or meaningless; emphasis on data collection rather than interpretation
Collaboration	Cooperative agreement inadequate, vague, or poorly conceived; no letters of support
Facilities	Equipment lacking, too old, or insufficiently robust for project
All sections	Poor editing; poor reproduction

ᵃ Adopted in part from E. M. Allen, Why are research grant applications disapproved? *Science* 132 (1960), pp. 1532–34. Reprinted with permission of the publisher, copyright 1960.

Applying for Grants

All agencies have rules for applying for grants. These include:

- budgeting guidelines
- page limitations
- dates for application
- university-based review
- preliminary approval before submission of a proposal
- number of copies to be submitted and modes of submission (e.g., electronic transmission)

The rules are the mechanics of grantspersonship, and they are important. No matter how worthy an application is, it will not be funded if it is not considered, and it will not be considered unless the rules are followed.

The federal government prepares application forms and booklets for all of its grant and fellowship programs. These materials, available through the sponsored-projects office, are often accessible electronically through the office's web site. The accessed materials will contain details on the application process. RFAs and RFPs provide similar information on federal grants and contracts, respectively. Foundations and industrial firms rarely have written guidelines for grant applications, but certain grant-making societies such as the American Cancer Society and the American Heart Association have published rules for grant seekers.

The published guidelines will address items listed above. Of note are budgetary restrictions. Some programs permit only the funding of graduate students' stipends, not tuition. Other programs may allow only operations support, or they may have a maximum amount that may be requested. It is wise to adhere closely to such restrictions.

Federal grant application deadlines are coupled to the federal government's fiscal year (October 1 through September 30 of the following year) and to review cycles that occur two or three times a year. NIH proposals, for example, are subjected to a two-stage review process (i.e., study section and advisory council), which is completed in nine months. Other granting agencies, such as the NSF, use slightly different review mechanisms; however, tough peer evaluation is a common element in all review processes.

Deadlines for foundation and industrial grants rarely exist. Grant proposals are considered at regularly scheduled meetings by foundation boards of directors or by scientific advisory boards of companies. These meetings are convened at regular intervals, and their times are available through executive officers of foundations or from contact persons at industrial firms.

Some foundations require a campuswide competition prior to the submission of proposals. This limits the number of proposals that reach the foundation and saves screening efforts. Personnel in a sponsored-projects office should know about such reviews. Internal reviews are also required when research involves animals, human subjects, and biohazards, as indicated in the previous chapter. The appropriate committee chairpersons or sponsored-projects office staff can describe procedures used at one's university.

Federal grant and contract programs rarely require approval prior to application. This is not the case with foundations and industrial firms. Researchers waste time if they send unsolicited proposals to these agencies. The preproposal inquiries noted earlier are important for foundations and corporations. Proposals should be prepared and sent only after receiving a positive response to inquiry letters.

Unlike publications, a proposal can be submitted to more than one funding agency. The duplication, however, must be dealt with honestly and straightforwardly. In the proposal, state that funds have been sought from more than one agency and that funding by one agency will cause withdrawal of the proposal from all others.

Researchers learn about the fate of their federal grant or contract proposals according to deadlines published in application guidelines or RFPs. The review cycle for grants is typically six to nine months.
There are opportunities, however, for intervening inquiries. Once a
study section or peer review group has been assigned to the proposal,
as indicated by correspondence received from the agency, it is appropriate to call the executive secretary of the review panel. Find out
when the study section review session is scheduled and ask what the
last day is for submitting supplementary material such as significant
new findings or preprints of papers. Once a written review has been
received from the study section, the executive secretary can be called
again for estimates on the likelihood of funding. These types of informal exchanges are common, and prospective grantees should not be
shy about making appropriate contacts.

Contract proposals are generally acted upon three months after
the submission deadline. Because of keen competition and the rules
governing contract awards, review panel secretaries will be less forthcoming than their counterparts on grant study sections. Complete
information on a contract competition, however, will be available once
a decision has been made on the contract awardee.

Review periods for foundations and industrial firms vary. It is
not unreasonable, however, to make contact with the prospective grantor
four to six weeks after submitting a proposal. The telephone conversation could begin with a polite offer to supply more information.

One has to be philosophical about grants and the grant proposal
and review process. I often suggest that once the proposal has been
sent to the granting agency, the prospective grantees should "forget
it," at least until it is time to make contacts with study-section secretaries. Additionally, it is always a mistake to count on a grant being
funded until official word is received from the granting agency.

The grant review process seems especially prone to human foibles
and the fickleness of sponsors. Virginia White noted aptly, "grant programs are subject to changing trends and modes not unlike those that
affect the fashion and automobile trades. Last year's best-seller may be
this year's white elephant, and the forces dictating the changes are
often mysterious and nearly always unforeseen."[1] However, success
will come with good ideas, effective proposals, patience, and good
humor. And success exceeds mere monetary benefit. The funding of a
grant or fellowship changes one's life. The resulting sense of independence reinforces the autonomy scientists need. The feeling of self-
confidence after a favorable peer review stimulates new levels of

commitment. These psychic boosts help ensure survival following the inevitable rejections that occur throughout grant-seekers' lives.

Successful completion of grant proposals can be an important step toward an advanced degree. The subsequent need to seek a postdoctoral or permanent position is discussed in the next chapter.

References

[1] V. P. White, *Grants—How to Find Out about Them and What to Do Next* (New York: Plenum Press, 1983).

[2] CBD Net (Washington, D.C.: Department of Commerce, current); http://cbdnet.access.gpo.gov/index.html

[3] University Departmental and Sponsored Research Offices (Washington, D.C.: National Council of University Research Administrators, current); http://www.crpc.rice.edu/ncura/sponsored.html

[4] Research Bookmarks (Fort Collins, CO: Colorado State University, current); http://www.vpr.colostate.edu/research.htm

[5] Office of Grant and Research Development (Pullman, WA: Washington State University, current); http://virtual.ogrd.wsu.edu/ogrd1/

[6] Grad Students Services (Pullman, WA: Washington State University, current); http://virtual.ogrd.wsu.edu/ogrd1/Grad.html

[7] Sponsored Programs Information Network (Guildeland, NY: InfoEd International, current); http://spin.infored.org

[8] Community of Science Funding Opportunities Database (consortium of more than 100 research institutions with headquarters in Baltimore, MD); http://medoc.gdb.org/repos/fund/

[9] T. E. Ogden, *Research Proposals: A Guide to Success* (New York: Raven Press, 1991).

[10] J. Dermer, *The New How to Raise Funds from Foundations* (Washington, D.C.: Public Services Materials Center).

13 | GETTING A JOB

> *We shall not cease from exploration and the end*
> *of all our exploring will be to arrive where we*
> *started and know the place for the first time.*
>
> —T. S. Eliot

Career goals depend on securing good employment. Obtaining a good job calls for planning and diligence. The job-hunting effort may require the equivalent of a few weeks to several months of full-time effort. The effort is aided by tips on planning, interviewing, and accepting offers.

Planning

Planning for the job-hunting effort should begin early in a graduate career. The planning activity is guided by the following questions:

- What do I want to do?
- What geographical location is desired?
- How can I secure a position to meet my professional needs and geographical preferences?

The choice of what to do is directed by one's graduate training. It may also be influenced by the job market and career goals. This is particularly true when choosing between a permanent job and a postdoctoral position. Some permanent university positions require postdoctoral experience. A postdoctoral appointment may also be necessary to acquire skills complementary to one's graduate background. Advice should be sought from an advisor and other trusted faculty on the necessity for postdoctoral work in a discipline. It is important, however, to know about the "postdoctoral trap." The researcher who stays in a postdoctoral position for more than two or three years, or who jumps from one temporary opportunity to another, may have difficulty finding a permanent job. A study by the National Research Council reported that "postdoctoral experience is found to contribute little or nothing in terms of subsequent income."[1] Thus, strong, lifetime, goal-related reasons (e.g., an academic career in many disciplines) should exist for choosing the "postdoc route."

A permanent position may be desired in academia, government, or industry. This choice should be based on discussions with faculty and friends located in these environments. An honest self-appraisal of the value placed on creative achievement versus service to others versus desire for financial rewards will help the decision-making process. You may also wish to consult the National Research Council's www site, Careers in Science and Engineering,[2] which includes descriptions of science- and engineering-based careers along with individual scenarios of researchers from the biological to the physical sciences and engineering. If one is unsure of choices such as academia or industry, interview opportunities should be sought in both.

Interviewing

There are several ways of obtaining an interview for desired employment, including:

- Personal contacts through an advisor, other faculty, and department chairpersons
- Contacts made at professional meetings, including "clearinghouses"
- Responding to advertisements in professional journals
- Use of executive recruiting firms

Large or prestigious departments are continually informed of employment opportunities through unsolicited mailings from industry, government, and academia. Find out whether notices are posted somewhere in your department. The chairperson may have other mechanisms for circulating employment notices to advanced graduate students. Find out what they are and have your name placed on the routing list.

Contacts at professional meetings are invaluable in developing potential employment opportunities. The widespread use of poster presentations at scientific meetings provides a good mechanism for meeting prospective employers. Because of the importance of these contacts, it is imperative to find a way of participating at one or more professional meetings during a graduate career. These meetings may also have clearinghouses where employers conduct preliminary interviews with prospective employees. This may require membership in the professional society associated with one's discipline. The clearinghouse service is one of the many advantages of joining professional organizations.

Job openings are advertised in journals and professional publications such as those listed in Table 13-1. Additionally, the www site Career Path.com allows searches of want ads in more than twenty-five metropolitan newspapers.[3] Use of the literature throughout one's graduate career will uncover other sources. An advisor may also be able to recommend unusual references.

Table 13-1. Periodicals That Advertise Openings for Researchers

Journal/Newsletter/Magazine	Publisher
Aquaculture Magazine	Aquaculture Magazine, Asheville, NC
ASM News	American Society for Microbiology, Washington, D.C.
BioScience	American Institute of Biological Sciences, Arlington, VA
Chemical and Engineering News	American Chemical Society, Washington, D.C.
Chronicle of Higher Education	The Chronicle of Higher Education, Washington, D.C.
Journal of the American Medical Association	American Medical Association, Chicago, IL
Journal of the American Veterinary Medical Association	American Veterinary Medical Association, Schaumberg, IL
Journal of Forestry	Society of American Foresters, Bethesda, MD
Nature	Nature Classified, New York, NY
Pharmaceutical Research	Plenum Publishing Corporation, New York, NY
Science	American Association for the Advancement of Science, Washington, D.C.

Executive recruiting firms may provide leads on industrial positions. Recommendations of firms may be obtained from an advisor or friends in industry. A list of executive recruiting firms has also been published.[4]

Before engaging a recruiting firm, ask for the names and telephone numbers of at least three people who have used their services. Call these people and ask them to relate their experiences with the firm. More than one executive recruiting firm may be engaged; however, for the sake of logistics, I recommend enlisting no more than three. Never allow one recruiter to handle your employment exclusively, even if asked.

Develop an understanding immediately with the executive recruiter that a curriculum vitae (CV) is to be sent out only after you have given permission. Some recruiters blanket employers with CVs in an attempt to establish priority on contacts you may have made yourself. Keep notes on all telephone conversations with recruiters. Map the progress of employment contacts. Have your notes handy when calls are made.

Executive recruiters handle a significant percentage of U.S. professional positions. In practically all cases fees are paid by employers; however, be sure to check. If a fee is requested, go elsewhere.

Many universities have placement bureaus. These are of limited use to graduates with advanced degrees. The bureaus may, however, serve as a clearinghouse for letters of reference. For a nominal fee, the bureaus will send letters of recommendation to as many prospective employers as you designate. This minimizes repeated requests for letters of recommendation. A bureau's letter-handling service may also be of value when changing jobs in the future.

Postdoctoral positions are frequently offered and accepted without an interview. This is good for neither the offerer nor you. If at all possible, seek an interview even if it is at your expense. A year or two of study under an incompatible advisor can be catastrophic. The guidelines elaborated previously in Chapter 3 can be used when choosing a prospective postdoctoral advisor.

Requests for Interviews

Interview requests are made indirectly through inquiry letters. A letter is sent in response to a personal contact or advertisement, or as unsolicited correspondence. Inquiry letters may have to be sent in great numbers, sometimes in the hundreds. Success with this effort, like that of a career, is dependent on the strength of applicants' credentials and their persistence. Excellent students find good positions regardless of economic conditions. Mediocre students always have difficulties, and they may encounter many disappointments during recessions.

An inquiry letter should express interest in the opening and the organization or institution. Refer to specific contacts or announcements. Tailor the correspondence to the particular situation. Never send a form letter or one that is handwritten.

Include a CV in the inquiry correspondence. The CV may be customized for the position; guides for preparing résumés are available.[5-7] In general, the CV should contain some personal data including one's social security number, which is often necessary to process interview expense reimbursement checks. Also include telephone numbers where you can be reached during the day and in the evening. Outline your education, research, and teaching (when relevant) skills, along with honors received. List your publications, including titles, and give names of three or four professionals who are familiar with your talents. Be sure to have permission to cite these references. Offer to have letters of recommendation sent and supply additional information if needed. The inquiry correspondence should be grammatically correct, free from misspellings, and reflective of your personality. Before sending out the first inquiry packet, ask for a review by an advisor and a couple of close friends.

Initial correspondence can be followed by a letter or a telephone call after a few weeks have elapsed. Sometimes things get bogged down at the employer's end and the reminder is useful. It is often true, however, that applications from highly desirable candidates are acted upon quickly, and the longer the wait, the less the chances of receiving a positive response.

Another way to follow up an application is to contact friends or acquaintances at the organization to which you are applying. Don't ask friends to give inside appraisals. These sources, however, can often indicate whether an application is moving along and when you are likely to hear something official. This quells anxieties.

In a perfect world, prompt acknowledgments of all correspondence would be received and quick decisions would be made on requests for consideration. Unfortunately, neither happens often. Additionally, one must be prepared for rejection shock. After receiving a number of turn-downs, applicants' self-esteem may erode to the point where they suspect that there is something wrong with them. Bolles suggests that this can lead to lower expectations, depression, desperation, and apathy.[5] Don't let it happen. I have witnessed the placement of hundreds of students in academia and industry. Success goes to those who have dogged determination and who are willing to expend extraordinary effort in the job-hunting process.

Invitation to Interview

Interview invitations are frequently extended during telephone calls. Become mentally and physically prepared for this possibility. Have an appointment calendar handy to anticipate discussions of interview times. Be flexible. Try to accommodate the employer. If given a choice of dates, plan to arrive on a Saturday or Sunday. This allows time for exploration before the interview and is particularly helpful if the employer is in a large and unfamiliar city. Be sure you understand permissible expenses before traveling. A prospective employer may not be willing to reimburse expenses for certain items (e.g., a rental car).

Preparing for Interviews

Make a folder for each interview. Include in it questions about the opening as well as personal information needed (e.g., housing costs, schools for children). Take notes during the interview, which will help you write down answers to the questions. As the interview progresses, use the unanswered questions as reminders for additional inquiries.

When possible, make a list of employees whom you are likely to meet during the interview. Practically all universities, corporations, and government agencies (including national laboratories) have www sites with personnel directories, which are readily accessible through search engines such as Yahoo!™ (e.g., College Select, alphabetically arranged hyperlinks to most major colleges and universities in the United States; http://www.yahoo.com/Regional/Countries/United_States/Education/Colleges_and_Universities/).

Once the list is compiled, obtain biographical information on each individual. University, corporate, and government web sites typically include hyperlinks to department or program sites, which usually contain biographical information on individuals you are likely to meet during the interview. Of particular importance are research and scholarly interests. Few things are more impressive to prospective employers than interviewees who are able to anticipate the interests and concerns of the employer's institution. If possible, try to determine the organizational structure of the interviewing unit. Make a chart of this structure as it is understood. Later, questions can be asked about the organization and errors corrected.

Prepare a short historical and geographical profile on the location of the interview site. Information obtained from encyclopedia sources and urban or regional www sites will be useful. This profile serves two purposes. It will make the trip more enjoyable, and it will provide material for conversations at social gatherings with less technically oriented people (including some upper management types).

Anticipate questions that may arise during the interview, such as:

- Why do you want this job?
- How are you uniquely qualified?
- What would you like to be doing five years from now? (Be careful of this one. If the interviewer's job is described through your answer, you may be perceived as a threat.)
- What activities do you like the most? Least? Why?
- How can you help our organization?

Be sure to understand what will be required during the interview. Many organizations request that a seminar be given on graduate research work. If one is interviewing for an academic post, a more elementary presentation may also be required so that departmental faculty can evaluate your teaching skills. Some universities provide a service to graduate students that involves videotaping a lecture given on the home campus. The resulting videotape is sent to prospective interviewers for preliminary viewing. I am not aware of anyone who has evaluated the pitfalls of such a practice.

Never ask to bring a spouse or partner on an initial interview. The question is presumptuous and should be saved for subsequent contacts.

Be aware of prospective employers' possible biases about personal appearance. Neatness and conservative dress are recommended for industrial interviews. It may surprise you to learn that it is still common in some firms to see only suits, white shirts, and conservative ties worn by male employees. Business suits are recommended for women and men.

University faculty are generally tolerant of different dress styles. Nevertheless, jackets and ties are recommended for men, and equivalent dress for women, when interviewing in academia.

The Interview

Job interviews give researchers and their prospective employers opportunities to evaluate each other. Interviews provide chances to convince employers that your skills and personality meet their needs.

You can influence the decision-making process by preparing thoroughly beforehand and performing well during the interview itself.

Be sure you know who the interview contact person is and who will meet you at the airport. During this first meeting, ask for a copy of the interview schedule and clarify apparent ambiguities. Begin memorizing the names of the contact person and people you are scheduled to meet. It is important to remember at least first names as the interview proceeds.

Be on time for all meetings during the interview. Continually show interest in the interviewers—their research, problems, and concerns. Ask questions from your interview folder, avoiding those that can be answered by reading materials you may have already received. Also, be sure to learn what is expected of the person who will be filling the position, and what benefits accrue. It is inappropriate to discuss salary unless an interviewer takes the initiative. It is wise, however, to anticipate a relevant question from the prospective employer by having a minimum salary level in mind.

The characteristics of a good scientific presentation have already been presented in Chapter 10. Some elements, however, are unique to presentations prepared and delivered during interviews. The audience may be a mixture of scientists, managers, and administrators. Pitch the talk accordingly. Speak clearly and at a moderate pace. Make a point of communicating enthusiasm for your work. If you are not enthusiastic now, how can prospective employers expect enthusiasm for work that is vital to their institutions? Point out the potential for additional investigations that were uncovered through your graduate research. This highlights creative abilities. Incorporate into the talk some of your philosophy and approaches to research.

Keep the talk to 45 minutes for a scheduled one-hour presentation. Repeat questions from the audience so all can hear them and answer each question directly. If you are stumped, say so. Honesty at this stage and throughout the interview is imperative.

During an interview, you will meet with your prospective supervisor one or more times. For an academic appointment, you will want to know:

- What rank is assigned to the position—instructor or assistant professor?
- Is the position a tenure-track one? What are the guidelines for promotion to associate professor? For tenure?
- Is the position a 9- or 12-month one? If 9-month, is there potential for a summer teaching salary? Or are faculty expected

to pay themselves from grants during the summer months? If so, how much can be paid for summer research—2/9 or 1/3 of the academic-year salary?

- Is it a hard- or soft-money position? (Hard-money positions are paid through a regular, permanently funded departmental budget. At a state university, hard-money positions are typically funded by the legislature. Soft-money positions are dependent on grants or other temporary sources of funding.)
- What are typical teaching responsibilities? Are there special accommodations during the first year to help you establish a research program? How are team-taught courses handled?
- What start-up funds are available for research? (In the physical, chemical, and biological sciences, it is common to request $25,000 to $150,000 in start-up research funds, principally for equipment. The request will require justifications.)
- What other resources are available? Seed grants? Technical help? Secretarial help? What about other support services such as libraries, information technology, animal resources, photoservices, machine and electronic shops? Travel support?
- What office and laboratory spaces would be made available to you? Ask to see these areas.
- What are the fringe benefits: insurance plans, retirement including personal and university contributions, medical-dental-optical care, social security contribution, educational benefits for you or your family, recreational or cultural amenities?
- What types of committee and continuing education (if relevant) assignments are common?
- What are the future growth and development plans for the department? For the college? For the university?
- Will the institution pay moving expenses? How much? What about house-hunting trips with a spouse or partner?

If an industrial position is being sought, the following additional questions are relevant.

- Are there bonus, savings, and stock option plans? How do they work?
- Will the company buy your house or condominium if you are unable to sell it in a reasonable period of time? At what appraisal?

- Will the company pay for interim accommodations near the place of employment before household goods arrive?

With federal government positions, explore the Government Service (GS) rules and how they would pertain to you. Throughout the question-and-answer portions of the interview, express empathy for the employer's position and try not to make your questions sound like a litany of selfish appeals.

After returning from the interview, send short thank-you notes to people who were kind to you during the visit. Be sure to ask who receives expense reimbursement requests and what types of receipts are required.

The Offer

Initial offers are frequently made over the phone. No offer is firm, however, until it is received in writing. The written offer should include information on the following:

- Rank and conditions of employment (e.g., tenure-track position and time in rank before being considered for promotion and tenure)
- Expected starting date
- Salary and benefits
- Description of financial remuneration for moving
- Contingencies (e.g., offer contingent on receipt of the Ph.D.)
- Special commitments (e.g., start-up funds, facilities access)

Seek an advisor's assessment of the merits of the offer. Try to answer written offers promptly. Ten days to two weeks is a reasonable time to make a decision. Stalling for more time can be detrimental.

With luck, you may receive one or more offers from which to choose. The acceptance letter will be easy to write—the rejection letter(s) difficult. Remember that it is difficult for an employer to receive a rejection letter after he or she has spent considerable effort to interview you. Be sure to refer to the assets of his or her institution and allude to any difficulty you may have had in making a decision. This employer is a colleague, and you are likely to interact again in the future.

You should anticipate finding a good position. Your career will be rewarding. I leave you with these optimistic prospects. Journey back through these pages as needed. Bonne chance and bon voyage!

References

[1] *Postdoctoral Appointments and Disappointments* (Washington, D.C.: National Academy Press, 1981).

[2] Careers in Science and Engineering (Washington, D.C.: National Research Council, current); http://www.nap.edu/readingroom/books/careers/

[3] Career Path.com (Los Angeles: Career Path.com, current); http://www.careerpath.com/

[4] *The Directory of Executive Recruiters*, 26th ed. (Fitzwilliam, NH: Kennedy Publications, 1997).

[5] R. N. Bolles, *What Color Is Your Parachute? 1995: A Practical Manual for Job-Hunters and Career Changers* (Berkeley, CA: Ten Speed Press, 1994).

[6] J. I. Biegeleisen, *Job Resumes: How to Write Them, How to Present Them, Preparing for Interviews* (New York: Grosset and Dunlap, 1976).

[7] R. H. Beatty, *The Resume Kit*, 3rd ed. (New York: Wiley, 1995).

APPENDIX: GUIDELINES FOR THE PREPARATION OF CONSENT FORMS FOR HUMAN SUBJECTS RESEARCH

The consent form should be a statement addressed to the subject and should read as such. Ordinarily, it is best worded in the second person. It must be in language the subject can understand. This includes avoiding or defining technical terminology, adjusting for educational background, and providing translations into other languages when members of the anticipated subject population do not understand English.

The checklist of points to be covered in the written consent form applies to all kinds of research although some points may not apply to every study. The checklist is numbered, but these numbers should not appear on the consent form. The consent form should include the following:

1. **A statement of the general purpose of the study**

2. **An invitation to participate**

   Points 1 and 2 can be combined in language such as "You are invited to participate in a study of . . . We hope to learn . . ." Such an invitation helps to communicate that there is a choice to be made.

3. **Why this subject was selected and how many subjects are involved**

   Example: Selected because he is a normal adult male, has asthma, or has relatives with a specific disease. This inclusion of subject criteria helps the subject assess the nature and importance of participation. If the statement of the purpose of the study identifies the subject population, it need not be repeated here. State approximately how many subjects there will be in the study.

4. **The procedures to be followed**

   This statement should include a description of the procedures, how long they will take, and their frequency. Use of randomization or placebos should be disclosed. If any of the procedures are experimental, they should be identified as such.

5. **Discomforts and inconveniences**

   Describe the discomforts and inconveniences that might reasonably be expected. For example, many studies use venipuncture to obtain blood specimens from subjects. A statement such as the following can be used to explain venipuncture to the prospective subject: "Venipuncture is a method of obtaining blood samples by inserting a needle into a vein in the arm and withdrawing a sample of blood. It is a routine procedure used to remove blood specimens from patients as well as healthy persons undergoing physical examinations. Venipuncture is accompanied by minor discomfort at the site of needle entry and may result in slight bruising at this site." If it is not clear from the procedure description, include an estimate of the total amount of time required of the subject.

6. **If there are any risks in involvement, a description of them**

   A subject at risk means any individual who may be exposed to the possibility of physical, psychological, or social injury as a consequence of participation as a subject in any research, development, or related activity that departs from the activities necessary to meet his or her needs. It also pertains to increases in the ordinary risks of daily life, including the recognized risks inherent in a chosen occupation or field of service. When appropriate, a statement that a procedure may involve unforeseeable risks should appear in the consent form.

7. **If any benefits to the subject can reasonably be expected, a description of them**

The suggestion of a benefit can be a strong inducement to participation. Thus, it should be limited to substantial and likely benefits. If the benefits to control subjects are different from the benefits to other subjects, this should be made clear. State that significant findings will be supplied to the subject (if they are relevant to the subject's health or well-being.)

8. **Treatment of physical injury resulting from research**

Subjects must be informed of the provision made for injuries that may result from their participation in research. If emergency medical attention for research-related injuries is arranged, a disclaimer for extended care should be put into the consent form, such as "continuing medical care and/or hospitalization for research-related injury will not be provided free of charge nor will financial compensation be available." If no provision has been made for treatment of research-related injuries, then this should be stated.

9. **Standard treatment withheld or alternative procedures available**

If any standard treatment is being withheld, it should be disclosed. If there are any other appropriate alternative procedures that might be advantageous to the subject, describe them. "Appropriate" and "advantageous" should be interpreted in terms of the spectrum of responsible professional judgment, not by the investigator's personal judgment alone. If the alternative therapies are too numerous to specify, a statement such as "Alternative procedures that would be potentially advantageous have been described" could be included in the consent form rather than going into elaborate detail.

10. **Confidentiality**

If data obtained will be made available to any person or organization other than the subject, the investigator, and the investigator's staff, the person or agencies to whom information will be furnished, the purpose of the disclosure, and the nature of the information to be furnished must be described.

Data in the form of tape recordings, photographs, movies, or videotapes require special attention. If they are to be made, they should be described even if they will not be shown to others.

Use of such data for other purposes must be disclosed and permission obtained in a special portion of the consent form. Final disposition of any such data should also be included.

11. Compensation and costs

If the subject will receive payment, the amount must be described or stated. If subjects receive services or treatment at a lower cost than would be charged nonsubjects, the reduction in cost is a form of compensation for participation. If there might be additional cost to the subject resulting from participation, this must be disclosed. When applicable, pro-rated payments should be described.

12. An indication that the subject is free to decide not to participate or later to withdraw consent and discontinue participation without prejudice

This section must not contain any exculpatory language (e.g., "before you withdraw, you must inform the investigator"). An example of a satisfactory inclusion is: "Your decision on whether or not to participate will not prejudice your present or future association (treatment, if applicable) with (indicate name of institution or individual). If you decide to participate, you are free to discontinue participation at any time without prejudice." State conditions (if relevant) under which the subject's participation would be discontinued by the investigator. Also, describe consequences of a subject's withdrawal from participation. This is particularly relevant if participation in the research involves treatment of a health-related problem and withdrawal would adversely affect that treatment.

13. An offer to answer questions

Include the name, phone number, and address of an investigator that the subject can contact if he or she has further questions and state that this information is for that purpose.

14. A statement that the subject will be offered a copy of the consent form

In all situations employing a signed, written consent document, the investigator must offer each subject, or her or his representative, a copy of the consent form. The reasons for this are as follows: First, it helps the subject maintain a continuing understanding of his or her involvement in the research and can help prevent problems should the subject forget that he or she has been informed previously of a risk or discomfort. Second, giving the subject a copy of the consent form helps the subject to recognize differences between his or her actual experience and what was expected. Finally, this contributes to preserving a good relationship between the investigator and subject.

15. Agreement to participate

There are several approaches to the language expressing the subject's decision to participate, for example: "You are making a decision whether or not to participate. Your signature indicates that, having read the information provided above, you have decided to participate and understand that you have the right to withdraw at any time without prejudice." If someone other than the subject is giving consent (e.g., parents; in cases of research with individuals less than 18 years old, the signature of only one parent is ordinarily required), the suggested language should be changed to: "You are making a decision regarding participation. Your signature indicates that you have read the above information and you have decided to permit (subject's name) to participate." Children who are capable of some understanding should be given an opportunity to refuse to participate. The best way to document that the child has been given this opportunity is to obtain the child's written consent, though this is of doubtful legal value. Alternatively, assent may be documented through a simple statement, "(name) provided verbal assent before this investigator on (date)," which subsequently should be signed by the investigator. In cases where surveys or related instruments are used, it is prudent to employ a maximum of two follow-ups to improve return rates. This limitation is advised to avoid harassment or feelings of coercion.

16. Signatures

There must be space for signatures and for the date of signature. If applicable, there should be space for the signature of one other person (e.g., parent, guardian), along with a space for the signer to indicate his or her relationship to the subject. The signature of the investigator is recommended in order to establish who discussed the study with the subject. If applicable, there should be space for the signature of a witness.

Sample Consent Form

You are invited to participate in a study of (<u>state what is being studied</u>). We hope to learn (<u>state what the study is designed to discover or establish</u>). You were selected as a possible participant in this study because (<u>state why the subject was selected</u>). There will be (<u>number</u>) subjects in the study.

If you decide to participate, we (or Dr. _____and his or her associates) will (<u>describe the procedures to be followed, including their purposes, how long they will take, and their frequency; describe the discomforts and inconveniences reasonably to be expected</u>).

(<u>Describe appropriate alternative procedures that might be advantageous to the subject, if any. Any standard treatment that is being withheld must be disclosed</u>).

Any information that is obtained in connection with this study and that can be identified with you will remain confidential and will be disclosed only with your permission. (<u>If you will be releasing information to anyone for any reason, you must state the persons or agencies to whom the information will be furnished, the nature of the information to be furnished, and the purpose of the disclosure</u>).

Your decision whether or not to participate will not prejudice your future relations with the (<u>institution or agency</u>). If you decide to participate, you are free to discontinue participation at any time without prejudice.

If you have any questions, please ask us. If you have any additional questions later, Dr. _____ (<u>give a phone number or address</u>) will be happy to answer them. You will be offered a copy of this form to keep.

You are making a decision on whether or not to participate. Your signature indicates that you have read the information provided above and have decided to participate. You may withdraw at any time without prejudice after signing this form should you choose to discontinue participation in this study.

_____

Signature   Date

_____

(Signature of parent or legal guardian)   Date

(This line should not appear on forms that will be given to subjects consenting for themselves.)

_____

Signature of witness (when appropriate)   Signature of investigator

INDEX